Programs for Asian Global Legal Professions Series Ⅳ

How Public Law Is Taught in Asian Universities

Edited by
KEIGLAD

✕KEIGLAD
Keio Institute for Global Law and Development

The publication was produced by KEIGLAD
KEIGLAD - Keio Institute for Global Law and Development
Keio University, 2-15-45 Mita, Minato-ku, Tokyo 108-8345 Japan
http://keiglad.keio.ac.jp/en/

Distributed by KEIO UNIVERSITY PRESS INC.
2-19-30 Mita, Minato-ku, Tokyo 108-8346 Japan
http://www.keio-up.co.jp/kup/eng/

ISBN 978-4-7664-2660-1
Printed in Japan

PREFACE

This publication reports on the outcome of activities under the Program for Asian Global Legal Professions (PAGLEP). It is a collaborative legal education program which has been promoted by partner universities in Japan and the Mekong region countries since 2016. We have attempted to improve the method of legal education by holding joint seminars and symposiums, exchanging students, teachers, and administrative staffs, and publishing the outcomes of those activities.

During the last term, we jointly studied how civil law, as general private law, is taught in Asian universities. The outcome was published as volume III of the PAGLEP series: *How Civil Law Is Taught in Asian Universities* in 2019. Following the topic of civil law, we have extended our attention to the topic of public law, especially constitutional law topics during this term. At the Hanoi Law University Summer Seminar held in September 2019, teachers and students from universities in Japan and the Mekong region countries studied major issues in constitutional and administrative law following introductory lectures on public law in each country. Next, an intensive discussion was held on the common topic of compensation for public takings, and the expropriation of private property by the government to conduct development projects in the public interest. This was followed by the Winter Seminar at Keio University Law School, where specific topics in public law were discussed during presentations by participants from PAGLEP partner universities.

This is the fourth volume of the PAGLEP publication series and includes the outcomes of those activities stated above. This volume explains how public laws including constitutional and administrative law are studied, discussed, and taught in universities in the Asian region, which has witnessed not only rapid economic growth but also the promotion of democratization movements. It will also contribute to comparative law and legal education by considering the legal development process unique to Asian countries. In this context, I hope that this volume will be used with volume I of the

PAGLEP series: *Comparative Legal Education from an Asian Perspective*, volume II: *Challenges for Studying Law Abroad in the Asian Region*, and volume III: *How Civil Law Is Taught in Asian Universities*, which provide useful insights on each country's legal system in the context of the globalization of law and legal education.

I do hope that the outcomes included in this volume will be shared by as many current and future participants in our activities as possible. The series aims to foster the global legal professions' abilities to solve difficult legal issues not only domestically but from a global legal perspective.

Isao Kitai

Dean, Keio University Law School

31 January 2020

CONTENTS

HOW PUBLIC LAW IS TAUGHT
IN ASIAN UNIVERSITIES

Chapter 1

THE CONSTITUTION AND CONSTITUTIONAL EDUCATION IN JAPAN

Tatsuhiko Yamamoto*
(Keio University)

1. The Drafting of the Constitution

The Japanese Constitution was written following the end of World War II and came into effect on May 5 (now, Constitution Memorial Day), 1947, six months after promulgation. The process of drafting and ratifying the Constitution has been a hot issue politically and legally in Japan since then.

On August 14, 1945, after the atomic bombs were dropped, the Japanese government under the "ancient regime," told the opposing councils, known as "the Allies," that the Japanese government would agree to the Proclamation Defining Terms for Japanese Surrender, or the Potsdam Declaration, which required the Japanese government to stop militarism, respect fundamental human rights, and embody the concept of democracy. The following day, August 15, 1945, became the most unforgettable day for most Japanese, because the emperor, who was the sovereign at that time, made a direct radio announcement that the Potsdam Declaration had been accepted and that the war was over. Like the anniversary of the end of the Pacific War, this date has been burned into the minds of the Japanese

---

* Professor, Keio University Law School.

population.

From the time the government accepted the Declaration through April of 1952, when the Treaty of Peace with Japan took effect, Japan was occupied by the General Headquarters (GHQ). At the beginning of the occupation, Douglas MacArthur, who was the Supreme Commander for the Allied Powers, felt that the Japanese government should change the Constitution drastically to be consistent with the principles of the Potsdam Declaration. However, the Japanese government instead wanted only to strengthen democratic tendencies in the existing Meiji Constitution and resisted changing the status of the emperor and moving the locus of sovereignty from the emperor to the people (popular sovereignty). The conservative nature of Japan's newly draft constitution shocked and disappointed MacArthur. He doubted the ability of the Japanese government to draft a more liberal constitution. He ordered his GHQ staff to draft the constitution with some notes, known as the "MacArthur Notes," containing the following requirements: 1. the status and authorities of the emperor were to be defined by the constitution, 2. war would no longer be a sovereign right of Japan, and 3. feudalism was to be abolished. The GHQ draft was influenced by other countries' constitutions, as well as ideas proposed by private Japanese citizens and scholars. It is hard to believe that the GHQ did not spend more than 10 days writing the draft, known as the "MacArthur draft," before presenting it to the Japanese government.

On the basis of the MacArthur draft, the Japanese government wrote a new draft constitution and published an outline of it on March 6, 1946. On April 10, 1946, the general election was held, giving suffrage to women for the first time. The final draft was ratified in the Japanese Diet on October 6 in accordance with the constitutional amendment process of the Meiji Constitution, and it became law on November 3.

There has been longstanding controversy in Japan regarding the political legitimacy of the current constitution, because it was drafted and ratified by the GHQ. Various right-wing parties and conservative politicians have strongly insisted that because the current constitution was written by a few Americans, and not by the Japanese people, it does not have political legitimacy. Therefore, they believe that we must rewrite "our" constitution without foreign influence. On the other hand, various left-wing parties and liberal politicians have strongly insisted that the fundamental principles embedded in the current constitution are good. They add that Japanese citizens were actually engaged in the process of making the Constitution. Therefore, in their view, we should not change the current constitution, but instead we must protect it against opposing political powers. Further, although the current constitution has never been amended, the issue of whether we should amend it has divided Japanese political society substantially.

2. Fundamental Principles and the Structure of the Constitution

As mentioned, the current constitution was established to break off ties with the previous political regime, because of perceived problems with that regime. These problems included the fact that there was an imbalance of political powers (the emperor was a supreme ruler), militarism could not be controlled, and human rights were frequently violated. As a result, the current constitution guarantees and entrenches three fundamental principles: popular sovereignty, pacifism, and respect for human rights. In addition, in order to prevent a political majority from amending constitutional provisions arbitrarily, the Constitution makes amendment difficult. According to Article 96 of the current constitution, "Amendments to this Constitution shall be initiated by the Diet, through a concurring vote of two-thirds or more of all the members of each House and shall thereupon be submitted to the people for ratification, which shall require the affirmative vote of a majority of all votes cast thereon, at a special referendum or at such election as the Diet shall specify."

To protect human rights and democracy effectively, the current constitution adopts a judicial review system. Article 81 of the Constitution says that "the Supreme Court is the court of last resort with power to determine the constitutionality of any law, order, regulation or official act."

Although the current constitution was designed to create distance from the previous political regime, there are some similarities between the Meiji Constitution and the current constitution. Similar to the Meiji Constitution, the current constitution has several provisions about the emperor. Of course, the emperor no longer has any political powers under the current constitution—the emperor is now purely symbolic of the State and of the unity of the People. The emperor's ritual authorities are thought to be derived from the will of the people, who are the source of sovereign power. In addition, the structure of the current constitution is very similar to that of the previous constitution in that the current constitution is also simple, short, and rigid. The Constitution has only 103 provisions in all and only 4,998 words. For comparison, the average number of words in constitutions all over the world is 21,960 words, and that in democratic countries is 24,430 words. There are many provisions that are very simple and abstract. The chapters of the current constitution are below.

CHAPTER I: THE EMPEROR (Articles 1–8)
CHAPTER II: RENUNCIATION OF WAR (Article 9)
CHAPTER III: RIGHTS AND DUTIES OF THE PEOPLE (Articles 10–40)
CHAPTER IV: THE DIET (Articles 41–64)
CHAPTER V: THE CABINET (Articles 65–75)
CHAPTER VI: JUDICIARY (Articles 76–82)
CHAPTER VII: FINANCE (Articles 83–91)
CHAPTER VIII: LOCAL SELF-GOVERNMENT (Articles 92–95)
CHAPTER IX: AMENDMENTS (Article 96)
CHAPTER X: SUPREME LAW (Articles 97–99)
CHAPTER XI: SUPPLEMENTARY PROVISIONS (Articles 100–103)

3. The Judicial Review System and the Court System

In this chapter, the Japanese judicial system is outlined briefly, before we examine the concept of judicial review under the Constitution of Japan as a safe-guard of the constitutional order.

3.1 Judicial system in Japan

(A) Courts

Judicial power is vested in the Supreme Court and in inferior courts estab-lished by the law (Constitution Art. 76(1)). The Court Act established four types of inferior courts: High Courts, District Courts, Family Courts, and Summary Courts.

The Japanese court system is unitary in two senses. First, Japan does not have a federal judiciary system like the United States does. Therefore, national courts operate in a single hierarchical structure. Second, Japan does not have a separate administrative court system adopted in traditional continental law countries like France and Germany. Article 76(2) of the Constitution prohibits any extraordinary tribunal that is separate from the judicial courts. Therefore, administrative cases are adjudicated through ordinary civil procedure, while special rules prescribed in the Administrative Litigation Act apply.

(a) The Supreme Court

The Supreme Court is the highest court. It deals mainly with final appeals against judgments rendered by the High Courts. Procedural laws limit the Su-preme Court's jurisdiction to issues involving important legal matters, including constitutional issues (Civil Procedure Code Art. 312(1)(2), Criminal Procedure Code Art. 405).

The Supreme Court has a chief justice and 14 justices. Most cases are as-signed to one of the three petty benches each comprising five justices. However, if the case involves an unprecedented constitutional issue or a possible overturn-ing of precedents, it must be adjudicated by the Grand Bench comprising all jus-tices (Court Act Art. 10).

(b) High Courts

High Courts, located in eight major cities, mainly deal with appeals against judgments at the first instance in each region. In those appealed cases, the High

Courts can review both factual and legal matters. In principle, a case is adjudicated by a three-judge panel (Court Act Art. 18(2)). The Intellectual Property High Court has nationwide jurisdiction over intellectual property-related civil cases. It is not one of the eight High Courts, but a special quasi-independent branch of the Tokyo High Court.

(c) District Courts

District Courts, located in 50 cities, mainly deal with the first instance of most civil and criminal cases that do not fall under the jurisdiction of Family Courts or Summary Courts.

In principle, a case is adjudicated by a single judge, although in a substantial number of cases, a three-judge panel is mandatory or discretionary (Court Act Art. 26). A recent major reform was the introduction of a lay judge (Saiban-in) system, in which certain categories of serious criminal offenses must be adjudicated by a lay judge panel, which usually consists of three professional judges and six lay judges.

(d) Family Courts

Family Courts, located in the same cities as District Courts, deal with cases involving domestic relations and juvenile offenses (Court Act. Art. 31–3).

(e) Summary Courts

Summary Courts mainly deal with civil cases involving claims that do not exceed 1.4 million JPY and criminal cases involving minor offenses (Court Act. Art. 33(1)). There are 438 Summary Courts across the country.

(B) Judges

(a) Justices of the Supreme Court

The Chief Justice is ceremonially appointed by the Emperor, on the basis of designation by the Cabinet (Constitution Art. 6(2)). Other justices are appointed by the Cabinet (Constitution Art.79(1)). Justices must meet statutory qualifications (Court Act Art. 41). Appointment is conducted in such a way as to maintain a customary quota with regard to justices' previous careers: six are judges of lower courts, four are attorneys, four are government administrative officials, including public prosecutors, and one is from academia.

The appointment of the justices is reviewed by the people at the first general election of members of the House of Representatives following their appointment (Constitution Art. 79(2)). When the majority of voters favors dismissal, a justice is automatically dismissed (Constitution Art. 79(3)), but this has never happened. The Court Act sets justices' retirement age at 70 (Art. 50).

(b) Judges of High Courts, District Courts, and Family Courts

Lower-court judges are appointed by the Cabinet from the roster designated by the Supreme Court (Constitution Art. 80). Most of newly appointed judges are graduates of the 1-year apprentice program at the Legal Training Research Institute of the Supreme Court (LTRI). They are initially appointed as assistant judges who are not authorized to sit as a single-judge bench (Court Act. 27). After 5 years of experience, this restriction is lifted almost automatically by the Supreme Court. After another 5 years, they can be reappointed as judges. Judges are appointed on a 10-year renewable term basis, until they reach the retirement age of 65 (Court Act Art. 50).

(c) Judges of Summary Courts

Judgeship at Summary Courts is different from the other lower courts. To be qualified for appointment, jurists must have passed the bar exam and either completed the apprentice program at LTRI (Court Act Art. 44) or have long experience in judicial practice and have passed the selection process by the Selection Committee for Summary Court Judges (Court Act Art. 45). In practice, a majority of Summary Court judges are appointed from court clerks approaching their retirement age, whereas others are appointed from retired high-court judges. The Summary Court judges' retirement age is 70 (Court Act Art. 50).

3.2 Constitutional review

(a) Concrete review system

Article 81 of the Constitution provides that the "Supreme Court is the court of last resort with power to determine the constitutionality of any law, order, regulation or official act." Scholars in Japan debate whether constitutional review under this article is limited to a concrete review or whether an abstract review is permitted. The majority view recognizes that the article adopts concrete review like in the United States, whereas others insist that abstract review like in Germany is also possible.

The *National Police Reserve* case is a leading decision where an opposition politician filed a suit directly at the Supreme Court, seeking a declaration of unconstitutionality of the National Police Reserve, the predecessor of the Self Defense Force (SDF). The Supreme Court dismissed the case without prejudice, holding that Article 81 merely confirmed the power of the Supreme Court to review the constitutionality as a last resort when exercising judicial power vested on courts. Therefore, the case or controversy requirement must be satisfied not only at lower courts but also at the Supreme Court. At present, case law interpreting "legal dispute" in Court Act Article 3 specifies the case or controversy requirement.

(b) Constitutional avoidance

In U.S. constitutional law, the doctrine of constitutional avoidance stemmed from debates over the proper scope of federal judicial review and the allocation of power among the three branches of the federal government and the states. In *Ashwander v. Tennessee Valley Authority*, the concurring opinion by Justice Brandeis assembled a "series of rules under which [the Court] has avoided passing upon a large part of all the constitutional questions pressed upon it for decision." Those rules, which are known, even to Japanese jurists, as "Brandeis Rules," evolved to modern avoidance doctrines such as the last resort rule, standing, and ripeness.

Because the Japanese Constitution adopted a concrete constitutional review system modeled after the U.S. system, the concept of constitutional avoidance is generally accepted in Japanese law. Actual examples are below.

(i) The Last Resort Rule

The *Eniwa* case is a famous example where the last resort rule was invoked. ("The Court will not pass upon a constitutional question although properly presented by the record, if there is also present some other ground upon which the case may be disposed of.") In this case, the defendants faced a charge of violation of the SDF Act and pled innocent because of alleged unconstitutionality of the SDF Act. The Sapporo District Court eventually acquitted them on the ground that the defendants did not destruct "defense property," but merely trivial chattels, which was not punishable by the SDF Act.

The *Naganuma Nike* case is another example. The residents of the town of Naganuma in Hokkaido filed a lawsuit against the Minister of Agriculture and Forestry seeking revocation of the Minister's cancellation of the preserved national forest in the town. In fact, the cancellation had been made upon petition by the Agency of Defense, which planned to build the new Nike missile base in the town. Eventually, the Supreme Court dismissed the case for the lack of plaintiffs' standing to seek the revocation, without deciding the constitutionality of the SDF argued in the lower courts.

(ii) Constitutional Avoidance Canon

Other cases have applied another avoidance doctrine on the basis of statutory construction. ("When the validity of an act of the Congress is drawn in question, and even if a serious doubt of constitutionality is raised, it is a cardinal principle that this Court will first ascertain whether a construction of the statute is fairly possible by which the question may be avoided.")

In the *Tokyo Teachers' Union* case, the defendant was charged with agitating a strike of public employees and the Supreme Court acquitted. The majority opinion construed the penal provision on agitation to be applicable to seriously illegal acts only and upheld its validity.

Although this liberal statutory construction was de facto overturned 4 years later in the *All Forest Officer Union* case, the technique of not striking down a statute but instead limiting its scope is still in active use. For example, in the *City of Hiroshima Anti Motorcycle Gang Ordinance* case in 2007, the Supreme Court rejected the defendant's claim that the penal provision of the ordinance violated Article 21 (freedom of speech, publication, assembly, and association) and Article 31 (due process) of the Constitution because of its broad literal applicability. The majority opinion upheld the constitutionality of the provision because from its context, it could be interpreted to be applicable only to acts by motorcycle gangs.

3.3 Recent constitutional review: examples

In the 50 years after the enactment of the Constitution, the Supreme Court struck down only five statutes on constitutional grounds, whereas in other cases it found application of the statute to the particular case unconstitutional. In contrast, from 2001 to the present, five statutes have been already struck down. Thus, it appears that in this century, the Supreme Court is more actively conducting constitutional review.

Two recent cases in which the Supreme Court struck down a statute were related to family law. In the *Succession by Nonmarital Children* case, the first sentence of Civil Code Article 900 (iv) was challenged. It prescribed that the statutory portion of succession for nonmarital children was half of the statutory portion of succession for the marital children. The Supreme Court unanimously struck down that sentence as violating Article 14(1) (equal protection) of the Constitution.

On the other hand, in the *Remarriage Ban Period* case, Civil Code Article 733(1) which set a 6-month prohibition period for remarriage only for women was challenged. The Supreme Court held that the part of the paragraph that prohibited women from remarrying for a period exceeding 100 days violated Article 14(1) and Article 24(2) (equality on marriage) of the Constitution. The majority opinion pointed out that the period exceeding 100 days had no rational basis to avoid overlapping of paternity of a child born to the divorced woman, whereas the minority opinion insisted that the prohibition period itself was unnecessary because DNA paternity testing was available.

Regardless of these two judgments, it would be still too early to confirm the liberal tendency of the Supreme Court's review. On the same day as the Remarriage Ban Period case, in the *Case on Surnames of Married Couples*, the Supreme Court upheld the constitutionality of Civil Code Article 750, which requires a married couple to adopt the surname of the husband or wife. The 10–5 majority opinion rejected the appellants' constitutional arguments on Article 13 (respect as individuals and pursuit of happiness), Article 14(1), and Article 24.

4. Constitutional Education

4.1 From Elementary School to High School

In Japan, "ordinary education," or 6 years of elementary school and 3 years of junior high school, is compulsory. However, most students attend 3 years of high school. The essence of the Constitution is studied in ordinary education as part of social sciences, especially as a "civics" class. Because it is difficult for elementary and junior high school students to read and interpret each provision and to consider the Constitution as a "legal" document, teachers tend to focus on fundamental principles of the Constitution.

Of course, in high school, students learn a little bit more, but in some high schools, students have to learn by heart and recite a preface of the Constitution as if they were memorizing poetry. They do not have enough time to study court decisions or contemplate how to improve the political system and democracy by using the Constitution. Therefore, it might be said that it is difficult for students to connect the Constitution as a law with real politics and to understand true constitutional theory.

As discussed above, there are two camps of opinion regarding the Constitution in Japan. The members of the first camp tend to think that the current constitution is a good thing and that we should protect it as it is. Some of them belong to the Teacher's Union. The members of the second camp tend to think that the current constitution is not "ours" and that we should change it. Whether teachers belong to the first camp or the second one is likely to influence how they teach the Constitution. In other words, even though biased textbooks and biased teachers are expected to be controlled and excluded by a board of education, we cannot clearly separate constitutional education in a school from political ideology.

4.2 Universities

In 2018, 57.9% of Japanese students went to university or college. Most employment examinations for civil servants in Japan include constitutional law as one subject, so many universities and colleges have a constitutional law class. Therefore, there are a lot of public law professors in Japan, and most of them belong to the Japan Public Law Association (JPLA). JPLA had over 1,200 members in 2018. What students in these classes study is quite general, though it is a little bit more detailed than what high school students study in their civics classes.

Some universities have a law department at the undergraduate level. Generally, a constitutional law class in the law department is divided into at least two classes. The first one is focused on fundamental principles of the Constitution and human rights and sometimes uses case law. This "Human Rights" class is generally assigned for the first-year students. The class is conducted once a week (each class is 90 min in duration), lasting from a spring semester to a fall semester (each semester has about 15 weeks). The second one is the "Government Structure" class. The class is generally assigned for the second-year students. The class is conducted once a week (each class is also 90 min in duration), lasting from a spring semester to a fall semester (each semester has about 15 weeks). There may be other constitutional law classes in the third and fourth years that focus on case law or practice of the Constitution. These classes are usually not mandatory. The "Human Rights" and "Government Structure" classes are outlined below.

"Human Rights" Class
1: On Constitution and Constitutionalism
What is the concept of the "State"?
Written and unwritten constitution
What is the concept of the "rule of law" or "constitutionalism"?
2–3: The Historical Perspectives of the Constitution
The difference and the continuity between the Meiji Constitution and the current constitution

The drafting period of the Japanese Constitution

The Emperor system

3–4: Fundamental Principles of the Japanese Constitution

Respect for fundamental human rights

Popular sovereignty

Pacifism: The meaning of Article 9

5: Theory and History of Human Rights

Declaration of human rights

Typology of human rights

Who can enjoy the constitutional rights? Juridical person? A foreigner?

Is the Constitution to be applied to a "private" company? Scope of the application

6: The Limitation of Fundamental Rights

What is the concept of "public welfare"?

How to balance human rights against public welfare or government interests?

Judicial standard of the balancing

7: A General Right (Article 13)

The right to the pursuit of happiness

The right to privacy (derived from the right to the pursuit of happiness)

The right to self-determination (derived from the right to the pursuit of happiness)

Cases

8: Equal Rights (Article 14)

What is the concept of "equal"?

Cases

9: Freedom of Thought (Articles 19, 20, and 23)

Freedom of thought and conscience

Freedom of religion

Separation of state and religion

Academic freedom

Cases

10: Freedom of Expression (Article 21)

The right to know

Freedom of the press

Commercial speech

Freedom of assembly and association

Censorship and secret communication

Cases

11: Economic Freedom (Article 22)

Freedom to choose one's occupation

Freedom to choose and change one's residence

Property rights

Eminent domain and compensation for loss

Cases

12: Due Process and Criminal Procedure

Unreasonable search and seizure

The right to a speedy and public trial by an impartial tribunal

The citizen judge system (started in 2009)

13: Social Rights

The right to maintain the minimum standards of wholesome and cultured living

The right to receive an equal education correspondent to one's ability

Labor rights

14: Summary

15: Term Examination

"Government Structure" Class

1: The concept of "Separation of Powers"

Traditional "Separation of Powers"/New "Separation of Powers"

2–4: The Diet

Representative democracy

Election system

Party system

The process of legislation

Bicameral system: The House of Representatives and the Upper House

Privileges of members

5–6: The Cabinet

Parliamentary Cabinet system

Powers of prime minister

The relationship between the Cabinet members and bureaucrats

The authority of the Cabinet to dissolve the House of Representatives

7–9: The Judiciary

Court system

The independence of judicial powers

Constitutional litigation and the judicial review system

10: Finance and Local Self-Government

11: Internationalism and National Security

12: Constitutional Amendments

13: AI Society and the Constitution

14: Summary

15: Term Examination

4.3 Law Schools

The path to becoming a lawyer in Japan was dramatically revised in 2004. Before that, we did not have law schools. We only had the bar examination, which anybody could take (the passing rate of the examination was about 3%, and the number of successful candidates was about from 600 to 700 per year). The old system had its pros and cons. The positive side of it was that because anybody could try to pass the bar examination regardless of his or her economic status, that was open and equal. However, in that system, there were few inter-actions between students, students and professors, and students and practicing lawyers. Because of this, despite the need for future lawyers to experience hu-man interactions and a "process" of studying, it was difficult for them to experi-ence these things and grow legal minds in a practical sense. Partly in reaction to criticism from academia, the government established and launched a law school system in 2004.

Since then, generally, students who want to become lawyers have to go to a law school in order to take a bar examination. Students who have graduated from a law department at the undergraduate level can go through a 2-year program. If they did not graduate from a law department, they have to go to a 3-year program, which is referred to as a "beginner" course. In a law school, professors are basically asked to focus on case law and to adopt a Socratic method, which is a form of cooperative argumentative dialog between a professor and students, sometimes between students and students. However, it is permitted for professors to adopt a form of lecture in the first year for the beginner course.

The current bar examination has two parts. The first part is composed of multiple-choice questions, including constitutional questions. The second part is composed of essay questions based on a precedent, including a constitutional chapter. Because constitutional provisions are very abstract and difficult to interpret, it seems that many law school students do not like to study constitutional law. However, because the current bar examination includes constitutional questions, some constitutional classes in law school are mandatory. These classes are focused on constitutional precedent mainly composed of leading cases and are taught using a Socratic method. Even though the passage rate for the current bar examination is higher than it was for the past examination (the current rate is from 25% to 30%, and the number of successful candidates is about 1,500 to 1,600 annually), we cannot say that it is easy to pass. So law school students have no choice but to study constitutional law with more care.

The Japanese government has been holding a preliminary bar examination since 2011. The pre-bar examination was established for a student who cannot afford to go to a law school because of his or her economic status, but the prerequisites for taking the examination are wide. If students pass the pre-bar examination, they do not need to go to a law school and can directly attempt the bar examination. As a result, many students try to take the pre-bar examination, and the number of students who want to go to law school is decreasing. This might be a flaw in the current bar examination system.

Keeping a constitutional democracy healthy depends on thorough constitutional education of students in a society.

Chapter 2

INTRODUCTION TO CONSTITUTIONAL LAW IN VIETNAM:

Constitutional Explanation and Review

Phan Thi Lan Huong*

(Hanoi Law University)

1. Characteristics of Constitutional Law in Vietnam

1.1 Historical development of constitutions in Vietnam

Unlike common law countries, the Vietnamese legal system is not divided into public and private law. The legal system of Vietnam includes many legal regulations wherein the Constitution plays a key role as a fundamental law. In other words, the Constitution has the highest legal effect in the Vietnamese legal system. All laws and regulations must comply with the Constitution. Since the establishment of the Democratic Republic of Vietnam in 1945, the National Assembly of Vietnam has promulgated five constitutions, which include the 1946, 1959, 1980, 1992 (revised in 2001), and 2013 Constitutions. Hence, the first Constitution of Vietnam was promulgated after World War II, similar to those of Japan (1946), Indonesia (1945), Italy (1947), Bulgaria (1947), India (1949), and the Republic of Germany (1949)[1].

---

* Deputy Head of International Cooperation Department of Hanoi Law University, and Head of Representative Office of Nagoya University in Vietnam.

[1] Textbook of Constitutional Law, Hanoi Law University, People's Police Publishing House, 2017, page 44.

The 1946 Constitution was passed on November 9, 1946 at the second session of the National Assembly with 240 votes in favor and two against. The adopted constitution marked the end of foreign domination, claiming the independence of Vietnam from the North to the South.[2] However, the 1946 Constitution was not officially published because war broke out 10 days after its promulgation. Nevertheless, it remained in effect in Viet Minh-controlled areas and in North Vietnam throughout the First Indochina War that resulted in the 1954 partition. It was later replaced with a new constitution in 1959.[3]

The 1959 Constitution included 10 chapters with 112 articles. It had some significant differences when compared with the 1946 Constitution. For instance, the economic regime followed the socialist model wherein state ownership enterprises played a dominant role in the economy and the government assumed a leading role in economic development under central planned orientation.[4] Moreover, the state president was assigned less power because under the 1946 Constitution, he/she only represented the country and the prime minister was the head of government.[5] To ensure that the socialist model was strictly followed, the People's Procuracy was established to supervise law enforcement and judicial power. The 1959 Constitution was established as the first socialist constitution of Vietnam.[6]

After defeating the French colonialists and US Imperialists in 1975, the Socialist Republic of Vietnam was unified. The 1980 Constitution contained a preamble, 12 chapters, and 147 articles. This Constitution had two new chapters on culture, education, science, and technique, which were prescribed under the chapter on socio-economic regime and the chapter on national defense—these

---

[2] Sự ra đời và phát triển nền lập hiến nước cộng hòa xã hội chủ nghĩa Việt Nam (the development of constitution in Vietnam), Ministry of Public Security, http://bocongan.gov.vn/vanban/Pages/van-ban-moi.aspx?ItemID=211, accessed 26 August 2019.

[3] Textbook of Constitutional Law, Hanoi Law University, People's Police Publishing House, 2017, page 59.

[4] Ibid, page 65.

[5] Ibid, page 69.

[6] Textbook of Constitutional Law, Hanoi Law University, People's Police Publishing House, 2017, page 71.

were under the political regime chapter in the 1959 Constitution.[7] Notably, the 1980 Constitution was strongly influenced by the former Soviet Union Constitution. The preamble asserted the status of Vietnam as socialist, and the legal system was defined as a socialist legal system. This was the first constitution to recognize the leadership of the Communist Party that was not prescribed under the 1946 and 1959 Constitutions (Article 4). Under core Marxist-Leninist ideology, socialist law, democratic centralism, and collective mastery were key principles of organization and operation of state apparatus. Socialist refers to supervision of power over administrative and judicial decision-making, which contradicts with the separation of state power propagated by the capitalist model.[8] The 1980 Constitution defined collective mastery under Article 3 as follows:

"In the Socialist Republic of Vietnam, the collective masters are the laboring people including the working class, the collective peasantry, the socialist intelligentsia and other laboring people, with the working class-led worker-peasant alliance as the core. The State ensures to constantly improve and consolidate the regime of collective mastery of the laboring people in all aspects, political, economic, cultural and social, throughout the country, in each locality, each establishment, making them real masters of the society, the nature and themselves."

Regarding the economic regime, *"The State leads the national economy under unified plans"* (Article 33). Under the central planned economy, State Ownership Enterprises (SOEs) were dominant factors for economic development. "Socialist notions that the state owns the 'means of production' to safeguard worker's interests."[9] SOEs played a leading role in the national economy and

---

[7] "Vietnam's 1980 Constitution," accessed September 23, 2019, http://vietnamlawmagazine. vn/vietnams-1980-constitution-4534.html.

[8] Hualing Fu et al., *Socialist Law in Socialist East Asia* (Cambridge University Press, 2018), 38.

[9] John Gillespie and Pip Nicholson, *Asian Socialism & Legal Change: The Dynamics of Viet-*

their development was prioritized (Article 18).

Under the 1980 Constitution, citizens' rights and obligations were similar to the ones outlined in the 1946 and 1959 Constitutions. Article 54 of the 1980 Constitution *"ensures the unity of interests between the State, the collectives and individuals on the principle of one for all and all for one."* Obviously, collective ownership was considered as a priority for economic development. However, the "one for all and all for one" policy did not encourage creativity among the working class because they were all entitled to equal remuneration. Hence, coupled with the collapse of the Soviet Union, Vietnam faced challenges in economic development. Consequently, the Communist Party introduced the Doi Moi policy in 1986.

The 1992 Constitution was promulgated six years after introducing the Doi Moi policy to respond to the needs of economic development. This was clearly laid down in its preamble, which stated as follows:

> *"Since 1986 our people have carried out a process of all-round reform and renewal initiated by the Sixth Party Congress and achieved very important initial accomplishments. The National Assembly has decided to revise the 1980 Constitution to meet the exigencies of the new circumstances and tasks."*[10]

The 1992 Constitution included a preamble, 12 chapters, and 147 articles. It was a turning point for Vietnam from a centrally planned and controlled economy to an open market economy that was socialist oriented. "The 1992 preamble [was] a delicate combination of revolutionary zeal and renovation policies."[11] Vietnam introduced a law-based doctrine under the 1992 Constitution without changes to the Confucian-socialist norm. Therefore, socialist legality remained a

---

namese and Chinese Reform (ANU E Press, 2005), 45.

[10] The 1992 Constitution, Preamble.

[11] Kanishka Jayasuriya, *Law, Capitalism and Power in Asia: The Rule of Law and Legal Institutions* (Routledge, 2006), 268.

key feature of the legal system in Vietnam.[12] The democratic centralism principle and single party policy were still key principles in the organization and operation of state government.

The 1992 Constitution mainly aimed at developing open market economy under socialist orientation. In other words, it was responding to new principles of economic development. Freedom of business and protection of individual ownership replaced collective ownership and SOEs. It became clear that to promote economic development, SOEs could not play dominant roles in all fields like they did under the previous economy. Therefore, Vietnam had to embrace freedom of business. This was the first time in the history of constitutional development in Vietnam that individual economic entities, small-holders, and the private capitalist economic sector were allowed to choose their forms of production and business, which were deemed beneficial to the well-being of the nation and its people, without any limitations (Article 21). In addition, individual ownership was guaranteed under Article 23 as follows: *"The legal property of individual or organizations shall not be nationalized. The State may, when necessary for reasons of security and national defense and for the national interest, purchase or requisition with compensation at current market prices the property of individuals or of organizations. The procedures for purchase or requisition are defined by the law"* This was considered as legal protection for the business sector, especially foreign investors. However, land still belonged to the State and individuals were only accorded the right to use it (not to own it). In addition, the State had the authority to distribute land to individuals or organizations for stable long-term use and only the right to use the land allocated by the State could be transferred (Article 18).

After 20 years of implementing the 1992 Constitution, Vietnam transformed from being a poor country to a low-middle income country in 2011 and achieved five out of ten Millennium Development Goal (MDG) targets.[13] Consequently,

---

[12] Gillespie and Nicholson, *Asian Socialism & Legal Change*, 8.

[13] "Vietnam: Achieving Success as a Middle-Income Country," Text/HTML, World Bank,

the Communist Party set five development targets for the period 2011–2020. In order to achieve these targets Vietnam needed to to carry out reforms in the organization and operation of government as well as judicial reforms. Consequently, the National Assembly XIII (August meeting session/2011) decided to revise the 1992 Constitution and, to facilitate this, it appointed a drafting committee.[14]

The 2013 Constitution was adopted to foster the development of a democratic society and a state bound by the rule of law. Under the influence of globalization and integration, Vietnam has made great efforts to reform its legal system so as to boost economic development and democratization. The 2013 Constitution includes a preamble, 11 chapters, and 120 articles. In comparison with the 1992 Constitution, there are some significant changes in the 2013 Constitution. For instance, it is the first time the term "human rights" has been adopted officially under Chapter 2 instead of citizens' fundamental rights and obligations (Chapter 5 of the 1992 Constitution). This new introduction shows the importance of recognition and protection of human rights in Vietnam. The 2013 Constitution also confirms the distribution of state power among the legislative, executive, and judicial branches, which is crucial in ensuring checks and balances within the government. The distribution of state power is provided for under Article 3.2, which states that *"The State power are unified and delegated to state bodies, which shall coordinate with and control one another in the exercise of the legislative, executive and judiciary powers"* (Article 3.2). However, the concentration of state power is maintained as a confirmation that Vietnam is undergoing a socialist transformation period. After the promulgation of the 2013 Constitution, the National Assembly enacted significant laws, such as the Law on Government (2015), the Law on Local Government (2015), and the Law on Organization of People's Court (2014), to facilitate institutional reforms. It is evident that Vietnam has made great effort in controlling state power through strengthening the

---

accessed September 24, 2019, https://projects-beta.worldbank.org/en/results/2013/04/12/vietnam-achieving-success-as-a-middle-income-country.

[14] Textbook on Constitutional Law, page 114.

judiciary, curbing corruption, and developing a more accountable and transparent government system. It is also important to note that it is the first time direct democracy, which allows Vietnamese people to participate in law-making and decision-making, is being defined as a constitutional principle. The right to participate in law-making is recognized by the Law on Promulgation of the Legal Normative Documents (2015). This law stipulates that the drafting committee must ensure active public participation by allowing individuals and organizations to give comments on draft laws (Article 6).

In general, Vietnam's constitutions have been amended several times. These amendments have been influenced by factors such as economic development, globalization, and integration. However, despite the amendments, the key principles of the socialist model, such as the democratic centralism principle and single party policy, have been maintained in all the constitutions.

1.2 *Key features of constitutional law in Vietnam*

Following the collapse of the Soviet Union, some researchers argued that socialist law had severed its links with comparative law while others were of the opinion that socialist legal systems were part of civil law.[15] However, Vietnam defines socialism and socialist law in her own way. Although Vietnam follows an open market orientation, it strongly confirms that the country is inclined toward socialism. It describes this inclination as a period of socialist legal transformation in Vietnam. Under the single party policy and concentration of state power principles, Vietnam's constitutional law is characterized by the following features:

– Constitutional law is a fundamental law of the legal system in Vietnam. The Constitution determines the key principles for the organization and operation of state apparatus. State organs are organized and operated under the democratic centralism principle, with distribution of state powers among the three branches of government (i.e., legislative, executive, and judicial power).

---

[15] Fu et al., *Socialist Law in Socialist East Asia*, 43.

Constitutional law also confirms the leading role of the Communist Party. The 2013 Constitution includes a chapter on human rights, which is a legal ground for most legislations and law enforcement mechanisms. In addition, the Constitution is regarded as the supreme law of the land (i.e., highest legal document of legal system) and all legal norms must be in conformity with its provisions.

- Supervision of the National Assembly is one of the most important features of constitutional law in Vietnam. Although the independence of the court system in exercising its judicial powers is guaranteed, there is no independent judicial supervision over the execution of the law. In other words, there is clear distribution of legislative, executive and judicial functions among three branches but without check and balance principle. According to Fu et al., (2018) *"In general, this tradition involved a set of non-judicial and centrally coordinated practices and institutions that checked and rechecked both administrative and judicial decisions for the conformity to the law and the commands of their superior."*[16] These features are absent in Vietnam's legal system.

- The leading role of the Communist Party and the way the state manages society are clearly influenced by socialist legal ideologies.[17] The Constitution provides the leading role of the Communist Party under Article 4 which requires that Constitutions, laws and regulations must comply with the policies made by the Communist Party. In addition, under the democratic -centralism principle that shapes the top-down model of state body. The central government plays a dominant role and delegates power to the lower levels, accordingly. At the central level, the government depends on the National Assembly and is obligated to report its activities to the National Assembly. At local level, the People's Committees (executive organs) are under the supervision of the People's Council as well as the administrative organ at a higher level, for

---

[16] Fu et al., 45.

[17] Gillespie and Nicholson, *Asian Socialism & Legal Change*, 45.

example the People's Committee at the district level depends on the People's Council at the same level as well as the People's Committee at the provincial level. Therefore, the administrative system is a hierarchical system in which the higher level delegates power to the lower level.[18]

– The Supreme People's Court exercises judicial power but without a constitutional review function. The National Assembly is the highest organ of state power and its Standing Committee has the mandate to review the constitutionality and legality of all legal normative documents issued by competent agencies. In addition, the Supreme People's Court does not have the power to interpret the Constitution and carries out judicial review power as Japan or United State model. Supreme People's Court can only provide guidelines for implementation the laws. In case of finding the regulations that conflict with Constitution and laws, the SPC can only recommend to competent agencies to abolish those regulations.

Socialist legality is the main feature of the socialist law. The Constitution of the socialist law is the highest legal document of the socialist legal system and all legal documents must be in conformity with it. All legal documents issued by local authorities must be consistent with legal documents issued by superior organs. Therefore, socialist legality creates a hierarchical system.

2. Constitutional Explanation and Constitutional Review

2.1 Constitutional explanation[19]

The common questions related to the interpretation of constitutions are as

---

[18] Phan Thi Lan Huong, Reforming Local Government in Vietnam: lessons learned from Japan, Lambert Publishing House, 2012.

[19] In socialist context and democratic-centralism principle, the term "interpretation of Constitution" is used as alternative for "explanation of Constitution" because the Court does not hold power to interpret Constitution and Laws. That why this article uses the term "Constitutional explanation".

follows: (1) How are constitutions interpreted and who has the mandate to interpret them?[20] Why do constitutions need to be interpreted? When a provision of the Constitution is unclear or can be understood in different ways when being applied, then a competent agency needs to interpret that provision to ensure that its application is accurate. Hence, it is important to ascertain the original intention of those who participated in formulating or ratifying the Constitution to unravel what their intended meaning was.[21] In some countries, such as the US and Japan, the Supreme Court has the mandate to interpret the Constitution. On the contrary, Vietnam is influenced by the socialist model and there is no clear distinction between the term "interpretation" and "guidelines for implementation" in the Vietnamese context. Since the National Assembly is the highest state organ that holds legislative power, only the Standing Committee of the National Assembly has powers to interpret Constitution. This is provided for under Article 74.2, which expressly states that *"Standing Committee of National Assembly holds power to enact ordinances on issues assigned to it by the National Assembly; to interpret the Constitution, laws and ordinances"* (Article 74.2). The interpretation of the Constitution refers to the explanation or guidelines for its implementation as depicted by the Law on Promulgation of Legal Normative Documents (Law on Laws, 2015), which provides that *"Explanation for the Constitution, Law, or Ordinance means a work of Standing Committee of the National Assembly meant to clarify the ideas and contents of certain Articles, Clauses, and paragraphs in the Constitution, Law, or Ordinance in order that they are known, correctly and uniformly applied"* (Article 3.3). The Supreme People's Court is not allowed to interpret the Constitution because of the centralization principle. Only the National Assembly and its Standing Committee are allowed interpret the Constitution so as to safeguard the status of the National Assembly as the highest state organ.

---

[20] Sotirios A. Barber and James E. Fleming, *Constitutional Interpretation: The Basic Questions* (Oxford University Press, 2007), xiv.

[21] Brandon J Murrill, "Modes of Constitutional Interpretation," *Congressional Research Service*, n.d., 10.

Contrary to common law countries, the interpretation of the Constitution in Vietnam refers to the explanations provided by the Standing Committee of the National Assembly; for example, Article 70, Clause 14 of the 2013 Constitution provides that the National Assembly has powers as follows:

"To decide on fundamental foreign policies; to ratify, or decide on the accession to, or withdrawal from, treaties related to war, peace, national sovereignty or the membership of the Socialist Republic of Vietnam in important international and regional organizations, treaties on human rights or fundamental rights and obligations of citizens, and other treaties that are not consistent with the laws or resolutions of the National Assembly." (Article 70.14)

The Standing Committee of the National Assembly issued Resolution No. No. 719//2014/UBTVQH13, which clarified Article 70.14 of the 2013 Constitution as follows: "The State President shall propose the National Assembly to ratify, decide on the accession to, or invalidate, treaties specified in Clause 14, Article 70 of the Constitution of the Socialist Republic of Vietnam."[22] This clarification is considered as an interpretation of the Constitution. Obviously, it is not similar to that of other countries where courts have powers to interpret the Constitution because *"much of the Constitution is broadly worded, leaving ample room for the Court to interpret its provisions before it applies them to particular legal and factual circumstances."*[23] Notably, interpretation is different from guidelines for implementation. However, both terms are used without any distinction in the Vietnamese social context.

Particularly, to clarify the terms "guideline for implementation" in Vietnam, many competent organs, including the government, its ministries, and ministerial level agencies (such as the State Bank and the Government Inspectorate) as well

---

[22] Article 2. Ratification of, decision on the accession to, or invalidation of treaties, Resolution No. 719/2014/UNTVQH 2013.

[23] Murrill, "Modes of Constitutional Interpretation," 1.

as local governments have the mandate to provide legal normative documents (legal regulations) for providing guidelines for the implementation of laws/ordinances. For example, Decree No. 43/2014/ND-CP was issued by the government provide conclusive information on several articles of Land Law. In this context, the guidelines issued by the government are different from the interpretation of the Constitution in other countries such as the US and Japan. In other words, Vietnam uses the term "explanation of Constitution" in legal and political contexts.

2.2 Constitutional review

There is need to distinguish between judicial review and constitutional review in the context of Vietnam. In general, the techniques used for judicial review differ from country to country, depending on adopted political systems. In general, judicial review refers to the control of the constitutionality of legislations enacted by parliament. Two models of constitutional review have been developed.[24] In the US, constitutional judicial review refers to the power of the court to review both public and private conduct to ensure that it is consistent with the constitution.[25] All courts have the power to conduct constitutional judicial review and the Supreme Court is entitled to make the final decision on whether any provision is inconsistent with the constitution of a federal state. The European model of constitutional judicial review has adopted a specialized constitutional court. The constitutional court is an independent institution, which is mandated to review the constitutionality of legal norms.[26] In France, constitutional review is the preserve of the Constitutional Council. The Council reviews institutional laws before promulgation. It also reviews other acts based on requests from competent persons such as the President of Republic.[27] Constitutional review can be

---

[24] Albert H. Y. Chen, Hongyi Chen, and Andrew Harding, *Constitutional Courts in Asia: A Comparative Perspective* (Cambridge University Press, 2018), 2.

[25] Theunis Roux, *The Politico-Legal Dynamics of Judicia Review: A Comparative Analysis* (Cambridge University Press, 2018), 15.

[26] Chen, Chen, and Harding, *Constitutional Courts in Asia*, 3.

[27] Constitution of France, Article 61, https://www.constituteproject.org/constitution/

carried out by different state organs. In addition, the jurisdiction of each model is also different from each other, as explained by Ginsburg and Versteeg (2013):

"Whereas the Austrian model only provided for limited jurisdiction of certain disputes, the German model introduced the device of the constitutional complaint, in which any individual could complain about the constitutionality of a statute or government action, even without a specific case or controversy."[28]

Contrary to the constitutional review mechanisms adopted by the US and France, under the *"democratic centralism"* principle, Vietnam has not yet established an independent model such as a constitutional court/council or a constitutional judicial review committee. The National Assembly is the highest organ of state; therefore, there is no institution that can exert control over it. Under the 1992 and 2013 Constitutions, only the National Assembly and the Standing Committee had the power to review the constitutionality and legality of legal normative documents, including laws, ordinances, decrees, and circulars issued by competent agencies. Notably, legality requires legal documents issued by different agencies to be in conformity with each other. Under the principle of democratic centralism, the legal system of Vietnam is a hierarchical system that requires legal documents issued by lower competent agencies to conform with legal documents issued by higher state organs; for example, a circular issued by a ministry must be in conformity with the Government's Decree.[29] The National Assembly holds powers to review constitutionality as follows:

France_2008.pdf?lang=en accessed on May 5, 2019.

[28] Tom Ginsburg & Mila Versteeg, "Why Do Countries Adopt Constitutional Review?" *University of Chicago Law School*, 2013, 6, https://chicagounbound.uchicago.edu/cgi/viewcontent.cgi?referer=https://www.google.com/&httpsredir=1&article=5621&context=journal_articles.

[29] Bui, "Law of China and Vietnam in Comparative Law," 160.

To exercise the power of supreme oversight over the observance of the Constitution, laws and resolutions of the National Assembly; to review work reports of the President, Standing Committee of the National Assembly, Government, Supreme People's Court, Supreme People's Procuracy, National Election Council, State Audit Office, and other agencies established by the National Assembly;[30]

And the Standing Committee of National Assembly holds the following powers:

(3).To oversee the implementation of the Constitution, laws and resolutions of the National Assembly and ordinances and resolutions of the Standing Committee of the National Assembly; to oversee the activities of the Government, Supreme People's Court, Supreme People's Procuracy, State Audit Office, and other agencies established by the National Assembly;

(4).To suspend the implementation of documents of the Government, Prime Minister, Supreme People's Court or Supreme People's Procuracy that contravene the Constitution, or laws or resolutions of the National Assembly, and refer those documents to the National Assembly to decide on their annulment at the next session; to annul documents of the Government, Prime Minister, Supreme People's Court or Supreme People's Procuracy that contravene ordinances or resolutions of the Standing Committee of the National Assembly;[31]

When laws or legal documents are found to be unconstitutional, only the National Assembly is mandated to annul those laws or legal documents based on the proposals of the Standing Committee of the National Assembly. In addition, the Standing Committee of the National Assembly has authority to suspend or annul legal documents issued by the executive branch. Obviously, the Supreme People's Court only reviews the constitutionality and legality of the legal norma-

---

[30] National Assembly, Constitution of Vietnam, dated 28, November 2013, Article 70 (2).

[31] National Assembly, Constitution of Vietnam, dated 28 November 2013, Article 74 (3&4).

tive documents issued by executive organs in the course of settlement of administrative cases. Therefore, the Supreme People's Court can only recommend to competent agencies to examine, amend, supplement, or annul legal documents when it detects that such documents are unconstitutional or illegal.

Article 6. Examination and handling of legal documents, administrative documents, and acts related to administrative cases

1. In the course of settlement of an administrative case, a court may examine the legality of administrative documents and acts related to those on which the lawsuit is instituted and recommend competent agencies, organizations, and individuals to re-examine such administrative documents and acts and notify it of re-examination results in accordance with this Law and other relevant laws.

2. The court may recommend competent agencies and individuals to examine, amend, supplement, or annul legal documents when detecting that such documents are contrary to the Constitution, laws or legal documents of superior state agencies in accordance with this Law and other relevant laws in order to ensure lawful rights and interests of agencies, organizations, and individuals. Competent agencies and individuals shall notify the court of results of the handling of legal documents recommended to be handled in accordance with law for use as a basis for the court to settle cases.[32]

The Supreme People's Court does not exercise constitutional judicial review powers similar to the ones adopted by the American model. In 1996, Vietnam established an administrative tribunal, under the people's court system, for reviewing the legality of administrative decisions or actions that are unlawful and violate the rights/legitimate interests of citizens.[33] Therefore, judicial review in

---

[32] National Assembly, Law on Administrative Lawsuit, No. 95/2015/QH13, Article 6.

[33] Nguyen Van Quang, "Grounds for Judicial Review of Administrative Action: An Analysis of Vietnam Administrative Law," Discussion Paper, Cale Discussion Paper (Nagoya University Center for Asian Legal Exchange, 2010), 9.

the Vietnamese context is a very narrow concept compared to other countries such as the US and Japan. The court only reviews the legality of decisions/actions of executive organs. This clearly implies that individual citizens are not accorded the opportunity to request for a constitutional review of any legislative laws or provisions issued by competent agencies. However, the court is mandated to recommend amendments or an annulment of legal documents in the course of settlement of administrative cases, as follows:

Article 112. Competence to recommend amendment, supplementation, or annulment of legal documents

1. Chief justices of district-level courts may recommend amendment, supplementation, or annulment of legal documents of state agencies at the district level or lower level; propose chief justices of provincial-level courts to amend, supplement or annul legal documents of provincial- level state agencies; and report to chief justices of provincial-level courts for proposing the Chief Justice of the Supreme People's Court to recommend amendment, supplementation, or annulment of legal documents of central state agencies.

2. Chief justices of provincial-level courts and superior people's courts may recommend amendment, supplementation, or annulment of legal documents of state agencies at the provincial level or lower levels; and propose the Chief Justice of the Supreme People's Court to recommend amendment, supplementation, or annulment of legal documents of central state agencies.

3. The Chief Justice of the Supreme People's Court may recommend amendment, supplementation, or annulment of legal documents of central state agencies on his/her own initiative or at the proposal of chief justices of courts specified in Clauses 1 and 2 of this Article.

4. In case the trial panel discovers at the court hearing a legal document showing signs of contravention of the Constitution, a law or a legal document of a superior state agency, it shall report such in writing to the chief justice specified in Clause 1,2 or 3 of this Article for the latter to exercise the right to make recommendations. In this case, the trial panel may suspend the court

hearing under Point d, Clause I, Article 187 of this Law pending opinions of the chief justice or suspend the settlement of the case upon receiving a written recommendation of the chief justice of the competent court specified at Point e, Clause 1, Article 141 of this Law.[34]

Notably, the 2015 Law on Administrative Lawsuits creates a new jurisdiction for the people's court—in reviewing legal normative documents. However, the court is only authorized to recommend to competent agencies to amend or annul legal documents. Therefore, the jurisdiction of the court in constitutional review is still limited because it does not have powers to decide whether legal normative documents are legal or not. In addition, many cases are found to be illegal but not under the jurisdiction of the court. For example, when Da Nang People's Council issued Resolution No. 23/2011, which limited the rights of citizens in resident registration, the people living in Da Nang province were not able to get orders setting aside this unconstitutional decision simply because the court does not have jurisdiction to handle such matters. However, this resolution was found to be unconstitutional by the Ministry of Justice.[35]

The Ministry of Justice of Vietnam is authorized to review legal normative documents (i.e., laws, decrees, circulars, and decisions issued by competent agencies as prescribed by the Law on Promulgation of Legal Normative Documents (Law on Laws, 2015)), as stipulated below:

The Ministry of Justice shall take charge and cooperate with the Ministry of Finance, the Ministry of Home Affairs, the Ministry of Foreign Affairs, relevant organizations in appraising the request for law/ordinance formulation before submitting it to the government within 20 days from the receipt of the

---

[34] National Assembly, Law on Administrative Procedure (on settlement of administrative lawsuit), No. 93/2013/QH13, dated 25 November 2015, Article 112.

[35] NLD.COM.VN, "Đà Nẵng hạn chế nhập cư là trái luật," https://nld.com.vn, March 1, 2012, https://nld.com.vn/20120229112858818p0c1002/da-nang-han-che-nhap-cu-la-trai-luat.htm. accessed 8 May 2019. (Strict citizen's registration of Danang is illegal).

satisfactory application for law/ordinance formulation.

(3) The appraisal shall focus on:

a) Necessity of the law/ordinance; entities regulated by the law/ordinance;

b) Conformity of the proposed policies with policies of Communist Party and the State;

c) The constitutionality, legitimacy, and consistency of policies with the legal system; feasibility and … of the proposed policies; solutions and conditions for ensuring implementation of the proposed policies;

d) Compatibility of the proposed policies with relevant international agreements to which Socialist Republic of Vietnam is a signatory;

dd) Necessity, reasonability, cost of administrative procedures of proposed policies (if they are related to administrative procedures); integration of gender equality in the request for law/ordinance formulation (if they are related to gender equality);

e) Adherence to procedures for requesting law/ordinance formulation.[36]

Although Vietnam has not yet adopted an independent model of constitutional review, it has its own unique mechanism of carrying out constitutional review.[37] Constitutional review is not only conducted before promulgation but also after promulgation by the Ministry of Justice (the executive branch), the Supreme People's Court, and the Standing Committee of the National Assembly. For instance, in 2017, 5.639 legal normative documents were reviewed by the Ministry of Justice due to their violation of jurisdictions, procedures, or conflict with existing laws.[38] However, the mechanism adopted in reviewing them was considered ineffective and inefficient. There are several reasons of the ineffectiveness such as the

---

[36] National Assembly, Law on Promulgation of Legal Normative Document, No. 80/2015/QH13, dated 22, June 2015, Article 39.

[37] "Cần Hay Không Hội Đồng Hiến Pháp?" accessed April 21, 2019, http://duthaoonline.quochoi.vn/DuThao/Lists/TT_TINLAPPHAP/View_Detail.aspx?ItemID=1009.

[38] VCCorp.vn, "Hơn 5.600 văn bản trái pháp luật được ban hành trong 2017," VnEconomy, August 9, 2018, http://vneconomy.vn/news-20180809065123316.htm.

shortage of experienced experts in reviewing laws, the huge number of substantive laws issued by various state agencies; the lack of legal database system.

Obviously, judicial review and constitutional review play an important role in promoting democratic values and ensuring that state powers are under check. Although Vietnam aims to build a state that upholds the rule of law and democracy, it still lacks an independent mechanism of implementing constitutional review. The rule of law is closely related to human rights and democracy, and the quality of the rule of law depends on the economic and political conditions of a country. Democratization is a process that requires a country to adopt the rule of law standards. However, "thick" or "thin" concepts of the rule of law are consistent with different economic systems[39] Vietnam is struggling to develop a comprehensive and consistent legal system; therefore, the topic of adopting a constitutional council has always been a controversial issue since 1992.

3. Teaching Constitutional Law in Hanoi Law University

Constitutional Law is a compulsory subject for law students at Hanoi Law University. This subject accounts for four credits, and it includes 30 hours for lecturing and 30 hours for seminars. This course is offered to first-year students soon after they join Hanoi Law University. Considering the fact that the Vietnamese legal system has been influenced by the former Soviet thinking, its constitutional law teaching methods are also influenced by socialist traditions. The precedents used in teaching the subject were introduced in 2016, after the amendment of the Law on the Organization of the Court in 2014.

Notably, there are no constitutional review cases because the Supreme People's Court does not have powers to interpret the Constitution or conduct constitutional reviews. As a result, the case solving method is not adopted in teaching

---

[39] Randall P. Peerenboom, *Asian Discourses of Rule of Law: Theories and Implementation of Rule of Law in Twelve Asian Countries, France and the U.S.* (Psychology Press, 2004).xviii.

constitutional law. The basic methods used in teaching include lectures and discussions, which cover topics such as the historical development of constitutions, political regimes, government structures, human rights, and problem solving (not case solving). In addition, legal analysis and comparative study methods are commonly used for assignments as well as final assessments.

A textbook on constitutional law written by professors of Hanoi Law University is the key teaching document for this subject. The textbook has17 chapters covering the following topics:

- Chapter 1: The fundamental issues of Constitutional Law
- Chapter 2: Constitution–the fundamental law of State
- Chapter 3: Historical development of the Constitution and legislation in Vietnam
- Chapter 4: Political regime
- Chapter 5: Policies on Economy, Social Affairs, Culture, Education, Science, Technology and Environment
- Chapter 6: Policies on Foreign Affairs, National Defense and Security
- Chapter 7: Vietnamese citizenship
- Chapter 8: Human rights and rights and obligations of citizens
- Chapter 9: State organs/government system
- Chapter 10: Election regime
- Chapter 11: National Assembly
- Chapter 12: State President
- Chapter 13: Central government
- Chapter 14: People's Council
- Chapter 15: People's Committee
- Chapter 16: People's Court
- Chapter 17: People's Procuracy

For undergraduate students, this course is taught for 15 weeks, with two hours for lecturing and two hours for seminars in each week. Handouts and reading materials, such as course description, assignments, and final papers, are uploaded online for students. Students are also required to participate in group presentations, and this accounts for 15% of the total course score.

In addition, Hanoi Law University also has other optional courses related to constitutional law such as comparative studies of other constitutions (such as the US, Japan, France, and Australia) and comparative studies of fundamental human rights.

To some extent, constitutional law is considered as a difficult subject for first-year students because most of them are fresh graduates from high school and enter into legal education with limited knowledge on the socio-political conditions of Vietnam. Therefore, it is necessary to create or adopt teaching methodologies that can encourage students to gain a better understanding of constitutional law in Vietnam.

In sum, the 2013 Constitution of Vietnam is influenced by both local context and global integration.[40] Although Vietnam has adopted an open market economy under socialist orientation, its legal system still displays key features of a socialist country, especially the principle of democratic centralism, which has shaped the structure of state apparatus and influences the hierarchical administrative system adopted (the top-down model). However, the legal system has reformed to respond to the needs of economic development as well as global standards, including the rule of law and good governance. Consequently, the 2013 Constitution of Vietnam, for the first time, provides a new chapter on human rights and distribution of power among the three branches of government. It is considered as a modern Constitution (the 21st century Constitution) that aims to achieve the MDGs. There are no case precedents related to constitutional interpretation and review in Vietnam; therefore, the case solving method is not adopted in teaching constitutional law in Vietnam.

---

[40] Bui Ngoc Son, Contextualizing the Global Constitution-Making Process: The Case of Vietnam, The America Journal of Comparative Law, Vol 64, page 931.

Chapter 3

AN OVERVIEW OF CONSTITUTIONAL RIGHTS AND HOW CONSTITUTIONAL LAW IS TAUGHT IN UNIVERSITIES IN HO CHI MINH CITY, VIETNAM

Luu Duc Quang[*]
Lien Dang Phuoc Hai[**]
(University of Economics and Law)

The implementation of constitutional rights has always been one of the core concerns in the process of developing a law-based state in modern democratic society. The history of constitution making in Vietnam reflects the development of human rights awareness of the ruling party and the state. All the five constitutions of Vietnam, since the 1946 Constitution of the Democratic Republic of Vietnam (1946 Constitution) to the 2013 Constitution of the Socialist Republic of Vietnam (2013 Constitution), have always guaranteed the protection of essential human rights. These rights have always been given a permanent standing in each constitution, such as in Chapter II - Basic Rights and Duties of Citizens of Vietnam's of the 1946 Constitution; in Chapter III - Basic Rights and Duties of Citizens of the 1959 Constitution; in Chapter V–Basic Rights and Duties of Citizens of the 1980 Constitution; in Chapter V - Basic Rights and Duties of Citizens of the 1992 Constitution; and in Chapter II - Human Rights, Basic Rights and Duties of Citizens of the 2013 Constitution. Consequently, this paper presents

---

[*] Lecturer of Law, Faculty of Law, University of Economics and Law.

[**] Lecturer of Law, Faculty of Law, University of Economics and Law.

an overview of the basic constitutional rights under the 2013 Constitution and the current implementation of those rights in the context of Vietnam. Further, it analyzes how the enactment of laws governing demonstration affects those rights with special attention being drawn to how constitutional law is taught in Universities in Ho Chi Minh City, based on the authors' experiences—in terms of subject contents, teaching methods, examination, and evaluation—teaching constitutional law for several years.

1. Overview of the Basic Rights under the 2013 Constitution of Vietnam

1.1 Basic rights in the 2013 Constitution

The 2013 Constitution of the Socialist Republic of Vietnam was passed on November 28, 2013 by the 13th National Assembly in its 6th session, and it became effective on January 1, 2014. The 2013 Constitution aims to facilitate the attainment of the country's goals during the period of transition to socialism, such as institutionalizing the national renewal policy in the new period; ensuring synchronous innovation both economically and politically; building the rule of law socialist state of the people, by the people, and for the people; ensuring protection of human rights, basic rights, and obligations of citizens; and perfecting socialist-oriented market economy institutions.

The 2013 Constitution contains a Preface and 120 articles, which are placed under 11 chapters.[1] The provisions relating to human rights, basic rights, and

---

[1] Eleven chapters of the 2013 Constitution are arranged as follows: Chapter I - The Political Regime; Chapter II - Human Rights, Basic Rights and Duties of Citizens; Chapter III - Economy, Social Affairs, Culture, Education, Science, Technology and Environment; Chapter IV - Defense of the Fatherland; Chapter V – National Assembly; Chapter VI - The President; Chapter VII - The Government; Chapter VIII - The People's Courts and the People's Procuracy; Chapter IX - Local Administration; Chapter X - The National Election Council, the State Audit Office; Chapter XI - Effectiveness of the Constitution and Amendment to the

duties of citizens are placed under Chapter II of the Constitution. This chapter's contents are as follows:

Constitutional principles of human and citizens' rights are underpinning legal and political thought, specifying the framework for the state activities into the legislative, executive, and judicial functions as well as for individuals in realizing their legal status. The 2013 Constitution establishes four underpinning principles of human rights, basic rights, and obligations of citizens, including: (1) responsibility of the state for individual rights; (2) standards for restricting individual rights; (3) unification of citizen's rights and obligations;[2] and (4) equality for right-holders.

Civil rights are also provided in the 2013 Constitution, including the right to have Vietnamese nationality; the right not to be expelled or extradited to other nations (Article 17); the rights of Vietnamese living abroad (Article 18); the right to life (Article 19); the right to security of the person; the right to donate human body parts and the human body (Article 20); the right to privacy (private life, personal, and family secrets, correspondence, etc.); the right to protect the citizens' honor and reputation (Article 21); the right to lawful residence of citizens; the right to inviolability of the citizens' accommodation (Article 22); the right to free movement and the right to choose one's residence (including the right to travel abroad) (Article 23); the right to freedom of belief and religion; the right to follow any religion or to follow no religion (Article 24); the right to freedom of speech and freedom of press; the right to access to information; the right to association; the right to protest (Article 25); the right to gender equality (Article 26); the right to material and mental compensation and restoration of honor of

---

Constitution.

[2] This principle includes the following contents: (i) equality – the foundation of the relationship between the state and citizens; (ii) the correlation of citizen's rights and duties; and (iii) the relationship between the individual interests, national interests, and other's interests in the exercise of human rights and citizens' rights and obligations. See LUU Duc Quang, *Nguyên tắc Hiến pháp về quyền con người, quyền công dân [Constitutional principles of human and citizens' rights],* (Hanoi: National Political Publishing, 2017) at 78–83.

the victims due to illegal acts of agencies, organizations, and individuals (Article 30); the right be presumed innocent; the right to a fair trial; the right to defense; the right to compensation for miscarriage of justice (Article 31); and the right to marry and divorce (Article 36).

The fundamental political rights are also enumerated in the 2013 Constitution, including the right to vote; the right to vie for election to the National Assembly or People's Councils (Article 27); the right to participate in the management of the state and management of society, and to discuss and propose issues to state agencies regarding their base units, localities, and the entire country (Article 28); the right to vote in referenda organized by the State (Article 29); and the right to lodge complaints or denunciations (Article 30).

The fundamental economic, cultural, and social rights in the 2013 Constitution include the following specific rights and obligations: the right to own private property; the right to inheritance; the right to compensation equal to the fair market value of the expropriated property (Article 32); freedom of doing business (Article 33); right to be guaranteed to social security (Article 34); the right to work (Article 35); the right of mothers and children in marriage and the family (Article 36); the right of children to be protected, cared for, and educated by the State, family, and society (Article 37); the right to health (Article 38); the right to learn (Article 39); the right to conduct scientific or technological research, or literary or artistic creation, and to enjoy the benefits brought about by those activities (Article 40); the right to enjoy and access cultural values, participate in cultural life, and use cultural facilities (Article 41); the right for citizens to determine their ethnicity, use their mother tongue and choose their language of communication (Article 42); and the right to live in a clean environment (Article 43).

Fundamental obligations of individuals subject to the 2013 constitution include the obligation to comply with regulations on the prevention of disease and medical examination or treatment (Article 38); the obligation to education (Article 39); the obligation to protect the environment (Article 43); the obligation to be loyal to the Fatherland (Article 44); the sacred obligation to defend the Fatherland, the obligation to perform military service and participate in building a national defense of all the people (Article 45); the obligation to obey the Constitution and the law (Article 46); and the obligation to pay taxes (Article 47).

The 2013 Constitution also determines the legal status of foreigners living lawfully in Vietnam. Accordingly, foreigners residing in Vietnam legally must abide by the Constitution and the laws of Vietnam and have their lives, property, rights, and legitimate interests protected by Vietnamese law (Article 48). For foreigners, the 2013 Constitution also guarantees the right to seek and enjoy asylum (Article 49).

1.2 Progressive constitutional rights in the 2013 Constitution

It is worth noting that the 2013 Constitution reflects a new ideological concept of human rights and citizens' rights, affirming Vietnam's strong commitment to respect, protect, and ensure human rights and citizens' rights, in accordance with international conventions on human rights to which Vietnam is a signatory and also the mainstream global context. Compared to the 1992 Constitution, the 2013 Constitution has some new highlights with respect to basic constitutional rights as follows:

First, the 2013 Constitution has adjusted the title and order of the chapter on human rights. The 1992 Constitution placed provisions regarding human rights under the fifth chapter titled "Basic Rights and Duties of Citizens." However, in the 2013 Constitution, these rights were moved to the second chapter of, which follows the chapter on political regimes, and they were titled "Human Rights, Basic Rights, and Duties of Citizens." This change inherited the structure of Vietnam's 1946 Constitution and borrowed a leaf from constitution-making processes across the globe. Therefore, this is not simply a technical adjustment, but it reflects the importance of constitutional rights, the principle of upholding the sovereignty of the Vietnamese people under the Constitution, and the supremacy of constitution-making power over legislative power.[3]

---

[3] HOANG The Lien, *Hiến pháp năm 2013 – Những điểm mới mang tính đột phá [The 2013*

Second, the 2013 Constitution no longer conflates human rights and citizen's rights as it was witnessed with the 1992 Constitution.[4] It uses words such as "citizens," "everyone," "people," and "no one" reasonably for constitutional rights and liberties. In the second chapter, there are 16 direct provisions on human rights, which are compatible with international human rights law and international integration policy of the state of Vietnam.

Third, while the 1992 Constitution only highlighted the state's obligation to respect human rights in Article 50, the 2013 Constitution asserts all the three obligations of the state, which include respect, protection, and the guarantee of human rights and citizens' rights, thus corresponding with the provisions of national obligations under the international human rights law. This not only ensures compliance with international human rights law but also creates a constitutional basis imposing responsibility on the government to adhere to its human rights obligations.[5]

Fourth, it is worth noting that for the first time in the history of the constitutions of Vietnam, the 2013 Constitution provides for the principle of limitation of human rights in Clause 2, Article 14, specifically as follows: *"Human rights and citizens' rights may not be limited unless prescribed by a law solely in case of necessity for reasons of national defense, national security, social order and safety, social morality, and community well-being."* The introduction of this principle is crucial in ensuring that the implementation of human rights and citizens' rights strikes a balance between individuals' rights and the state's obligations

Constitution: The Breakthrough New Points], (Hanoi: Judicial Publishing House, 2015) at 20–22.

[4] Article 50 of the 1992 Constitution provides: *"In the Socialist Republic of Vietnam, human rights in all respects, political, civic, economic, cultural and social are respected, find their expression in the rights of citizens and are provided for by the Constitution and the law."*

[5] Văn phòng thường trực về nhân quyền – Học viện Chính trị quốc gia Hồ Chí Minh (Permanent office on Human rights - Ho Chi Minh National Academy of Politics), *Quyền con người, quyền và nghĩa vụ cơ bản của công dân trong Hiến pháp Việt Nam [Human rights, Basic Rights and Duties of Citizens in Vietnam's Constitutions]*, Hà Nội, 2015 at 206.

and ensures that such relationships are healthy and transparent.[6]

Last but not least, the 2013 Constitution not only preserves provisions regarding human rights already enshrined in the previous constitution but it also recognizes several new rights, including the citizens' right against being expelled or extradited to another state (Article 17); the right to life (Article 19); the right to legal residence of citizens (Article 22); the right to social security of citizens (Article 34); the right to enjoy and access cultural heritage, participate in cultural life and make use of cultural facilities (Article 41); citizens' right to determine nationality, use their mother language, and selecting their language of communication (Article 42); and the right to a clean environment (Article 43).

2. Mechanisms for Implementation of Constitutional Rights in Vietnam through the Lens of Demonstration Cases

2.1 The practice of protests and the process of building the law on demonstrations from 2011 till now

The right to protest is one of Vietnamese citizens' fundamental rights set forth in Article 25 of the 1959 Constitution, Article 67 of the 1980 Constitution, Article 69 of the 1992 Constitution, and Article 25 of the 2013 Constitution. Consequently, this chapter analyzes some notable demonstrations in Vietnam as well as the procedures followed in making laws governing protests from 2011 until now.

From June to August 2011, aggressive and infringement behaviors of the Chinese government, which posed a threat and violation of Vietnam's sovereignty over the East Sea, were witnessed. As a result, they provoked some serious spon-

---

[6] Viện Khoa học pháp lý (Institute of Legal Science), *Bình luận khoa học Hiến pháp hiện hành (năm 2013) [Scientific Commentaries on the current Constitution (2013)]*, (Hanoi: National Political Publishing, 2018) at 119.

taneous protests among Vietnamese citizens against the Chinese government. Major protests mainly took place in the center of Hanoi and Ho Chi Minh City. These events caught the attention of the general public, and they also showed passive and disconcerted reactions of the authorities in handling such protests. Accordingly, the Government's Decree No. 38/2005/ND-CP, which stipulates a number of measures to ensure public order, and the Circular of the Minister of Public Security No. 09/2005/TT-BCA, which provides guidelines on the implementation of a number of articles of Decree No. 38/2005/ND-CP, were often used as a legal basis to handle similar protest cases. However, there is no clear definition of "protest" in both documents but the concept of "crowding" is repeated 21 times.

In November 2011, the Prime Minister, Nguyen Tan Dung, officially proposed that the National Assembly incorporates the Law on Protests into the law and ordinance building program of the XIIIth National Assembly. The Law on Protests not only ensures compliance with constitutional provisions but also greatly matches with cultural-historical characteristics, specific characteristics of the Vietnamese people, international human rights standards, and ensures citizens' democratic freedom. Moreover, this law can be considered as a measure to prevent acts that infringe upon the security of order and the interests of society and individuals. The National Assembly deputies initiated aggressive discussions over this issue in their late 2011 meetings. Apart from those viewpoints that concurred with the Prime Minister's proposals, many delegates expressed opposition citing reasons such as protests were infamy and synonymous with vandalism as well as violence, especially when it comes to people with low levels of awareness who should not be given the right to protest. Besides, protests were not suitable for the one-party monarchy in Vietnam and caused political instability.[7]

On May 30, 2014, the 7th session rubberstamped the coming into force of the

---

[7] LUU Duc Quang, *"Quyền và nghĩa vụ của công dân do Hiến pháp và luật quy định" – nhận diện từ lý luận và tình huống ["Citizens' rights and obligations are prescribed by the Constitution and laws" - identified from theory and situations]*, Tap chi Nghien Cuu Lap Phap [Journal of Legislative Studies] (2013) 14, at 16–24.

2013 Constitution five months after its enactment and after the delegates had a lot of serious discussions about the need for the Law on Protests. Eventually, the XIIIth National Assembly voted to adopt the resolution on the law and ordinance building program 2015. As such, the Law on Protests proposal was deliberated during the 9th meeting (May 2015) and voted for approval during the 10th meeting (October 2015)[8]. On June 9, 2015, during the 9th session (15 months after the 2013 Constitution officially coming into effect), the National Assembly voted to pass the resolution on the law and ordinance building program in 2016. Subsequently, the Law on Protests proposal was discussed during the 11th session (March 2016) and approved during the 2nd session of the XIV National Assembly (October 2016)[9].

On June 9, 2018, the National Assembly's Portal issued a press release proposing what should be included in the law on special administrative-economic zones, which was being considered by the National Assembly during the 5th session of the XIV National Assembly. Accordingly, in the law and ordinance building program 2018, during the 5th session, the National Assembly discussed and commented on Van Don, Bac Van Phong, and Phu Quoc's proposals on the law on special administrative-economic zones. After receiving different perspectives from the National Assembly deputies and people from all social strata, the National Assembly's Standing Committee cautiously considered many aspects and then agreed with the government to amend the proposed laws to ensure that that there will be no special cases as pertains to the term of land use for production and business and the maximum term was not longer than 99 years. The proposed law was still under consideration by the National Assembly and there was a chance that it could be approved during the 6th session of the XIV National As-

---

[8] Chung Hoang, *Cuối năm 2015 có luật biểu tình [The law on demonstrations will be completed at the end of 2015]*, VIETNAMNET.VN, (June 1, 2015), http://vietnamnet.vn/vn/chinh-tri/178391/cuoi-2015-co-luat-bieu-tinh.html.

[9] Minh Thuy, *Quốc hội đồng ý lùi luật biểu tình [The National Assembly agreed to put off the law on demonstrations]*, VNECONOMY.VN, (June 6, 2015), http://vneconomy.vn/thoi-su/quoc-hoi-dong-y-lui-luat-bieu-tinh-20150609083845209.htm.

sembly (October 2018)[10].

On June 10, 2018, thousands of people took to the streets in Hanoi, Da Nang, Binh Thuan, Nha Trang, Binh Duong, Dong Nai, Vung Tau, and Ho Chi Minh City to protest two bills (one on special administrative-economic zones and the other one on cyber security) that were being discussed by the National Assembly. Violence, anti-law enforcement, and property destruction were witnessed in some areas of the country. The National Assembly had to vote on the withdrawal of the proposed law on approval and resolution on the implementation of the law on special administrative-economic zones (in Van Don, Bac Van Phong, and Phu Quoc). However, during the 6th session of the XIVth National Assembly, the bill was passed into law with an approval proportion of 85.63%[11]. On June 12, 2018, the National Assembly voted to approve the Law on Cyber Security, with 86.86% of the members approving the bill.[12] The National Assembly deputies continued to propose the need for the Law on Protests that could allow people to adequately express their views in the right place and provide the authorities with a legal basis to control and manage aggressive groups[13].

On April 10, 2019, during discussions on the law and ordinance building pro-

---

[10] *Trình Quốc hội xem xét lùi thời gian thông qua luật đặc khu [Submitting to the National Assembly for delaying the approval of the proposed law on special economic zones]*, TUOI-TRE.VN, (June 9, 2018), https://tuoitre.vn/trinh-quoc-hoi-xem-xet-lui-thoi-gian-thong-qua-luat-dac-khu-20180609150727511.htm.

[11] Vo Hai – Anh Minh, *Chủ tịch Quốc hội kêu gọi mọi người dân bình tĩnh tin vào quyết định của nhà nước, [Chairman of the National Assembly asks people to calm down and believe in the State's decision]*, VNEXPRESS.NET, (June 11, 2018), https://vnexpress.net/thoi-su/chu-tich-quoc-hoi-keu-goi-nguoi-dan-binh-tinh-tin-vao-quyet-dinh-cua-nha-nuoc-3761759.html.

[12] Bao Ha, *Quốc hội thông qua Luật An ninh mạng với hơn 86 đại biểu tán thành [The National Assembly passes the Cyber Security Law with more than 86% of agreed votes]*, (June 12, 2018), VNEXPRESS.NET, https://vnexpress.net/phap-luat/quoc-hoi-thong-qua-luat-an-ninh-mang-voi-hon-86-dai-bieu-tan-thanh-3762314.html.

[13] Ba Chiem – Thang Quang, *Cần có luật biểu tình để phân tách người kích động, quá khích [The law on demonstrations is needed to separate violent and aggressive people]*, NEWS. ZING.VN, (June 11, 2018), https://news.zing.vn/can-co-luat-bieu-tinh-de-phan-tach-nguoi-kich-dong-qua-khich-post850415.html.

gram in 2020 at the 33rd meeting of the National Assembly Standing Committee, Mr. Le Thanh Long, the Minister of Justice, stated that "the proposal of Law on protest was being studied and improved carefully in terms of theoretical and legal basis by Ministry of Public Security relevant authorities. Moreover, some surveys were conducted in localities, which aims not only to build practically the regulations of Law on Protest, ensure the implementation of human rights, rights and obligations of citizens but also to avoid our enemies taking advantage of protests to disrupt order and fighting against the Vietnamese Communist Party and the Vietnamese State"[14].

On September 11, 2019, the Standing Committee of the National Assembly commented on the preliminary report on 05 years of implementing the 2013 Constitution (2014–2019). Uong Chu Luu, the Deputy Chairman of the National Assembly, observed that "In the Government report, we currently have 03 kind of laws which are already in the plan but not yet enacted: Law on Association, Law on protest, Law on blood donation. It is indisputable that these are human rights and civil rights prescribed in constitutional law, so please give us your analysis and settle a plan of enactment, not to procrastinate any more"[15]. Therefore, the enactment of the Law on Protests has not been implemented yet and is still being procrastinated.

2.2 Analyzing the mechanisms of implementing Constitutional rights

First, the reasons for "suspending" or "omitting" some rights that are regulated in constitutional law. Even though there are many factors attributed

---

[14] P.Thao, *Chinh lý luật đơn vị hành chính, kinh tế đặc biệt theo hướng luật chung [Revised the law on special administrative - economic zones toward a general law]* DANTRI.COM, (April 10, 2019), https://dantri.com.vn/xa-hoi/chinh-ly-luat-don-vi-hanh-chinh-kinh-te-dac-biet-theo-huong-luat-chung-20190410110600376.htm.

[15] Le Kien, *Tại sao chưa ban hành được luật biểu tình? [Why has the law on demonstrations been not enacted?]*, TUOITRE.VN, (September 11, 2019), https://tuoitre.vn/tai-sao-chua-ban-hanh-duoc-luat-bieu-tinh-20190911144615061.htm?fbclid=IwAR0ita3bG4Eo6OogATxE-W_T0TNThr0uT8ANqoGg1244iAz2Y3urSnf8QiQ.

to this problem,[16] one of the most fundamental roots is the management think-ing of the Vietnamese authorities. Upon analyzing the current situation, there are two aspects of thinking: First, from the viewpoint of executive authorities, they have not formulated a concrete legal foundation for managing a variety of scenarios that may arise due to citizens exercising their constitutional rights. In-stead, they tend to implement passive management. Second, from the legislators' perspective, they often fall into the following traps: (1) "Thinking on behalf of the executive," worrying that the laws that they pass with sections considered "sensitive" might be exploited and cause friction between the legislature and the executive as the executive seeks to ensure political security. This way of thinking gives rise to an interesting situation whereby the legislators' tendency to consid-er the executive's views slows down the making of laws that the executive branch itself works hard to promote in public. (2) "Thinking on behalf of citizens" to ensure that their rights are provided for and protected. Accordingly, the public authority's attitude toward citizens' rights to protest also reflects its respect for the Constitution and its level of legal knowledge in the law-based state, in which citizens can do everything that the law does not prohibit. Nevertheless, this spirit has not been expressed much in the 2013 Constitution.[17] Therefore, it is neces-sary to impose legal responsibilities on Vietnamese public agencies when they promulgate or delay the enactment of laws to concretize constitutional rights without bona fide reasons, causing damage or threatening to harm the legitimate

---

[16] This also happens to the right to nationalize with fair market value compensation in the context of the 1992 Constitution. Accordingly, Article 23 of the 1992 Constitution states, "the lawful property of individuals and organizations shall not be nationalized. In cases made necessary because of national defense, security and the national interest, the State can make a forcible purchase of or can requisition pieces of property of individuals or organizations against compensation, taking into account current market prices. The formalities of the for-cible purchase or requisition shall be determined by law." However, it was not until 2008 that the 12th National Assembly promulgated the law on compulsorily purchase and requisition of the property.

[17] This spirit is only expressed in Article 33 of the 2013 Constitution, specifically as follows: "everyone has the right to freedom of business in the trades that are not prohibited by law."

rights and interests of citizens as well as reducing the all-round development of the society.[18]

Second is the principle of the immediate effect of constitutional rights and the need to legislate constitutional rights. According to Tran Thanh Huong, for countries in which their Constitution has direct legal effect (recognizing the principle of direct effect of constitutional rights), courts may rely on the principles of law to settle disputes over enforcing constitutional rights, even if there are no particular regulations that concretize those constitutional rights. In Vietnam, *"if a right is not specifically stated in the sub-law guiding documents, authorities often refuse to apply laws to protect citizens' rights. Even if required, for example, the Court will send the requirement back, or procrastinate the procedure by explaining that they have to wait for instructions from the Supreme People's Court ..."*[19] In terms of linguistic development in the Constitution, the wording *"Everyone has/Citizens have rights ... according to legislation/ law"* in the 1992 Constitution was changed to *"Everyone has/Citizens have rights ... the implementation of these rights in accordance with legislations/law"* in the 2013 Constitution. This is a significant change in the Vietnamese lawmakers' ideology, which implies that human rights shall be recognized by the state rather than being bestowed by the state. However, this wording is still not sufficient enough to eliminate the risk of violation of constitutional rights by omission or failure to act by the State without a guaranteed mechanism as alluded above. In reality, if there is no detailed guidance and mechanisms on implementing constitutional rights, then such rights will not be fully implemented. In discussing this issue, Dr. Nguyen Minh Doan observed that *"There is a problem that whereas by-law*

---

[18] Mai Van Thang, *"Trách nhiệm Hiến pháp trong bối cảnh cải cách pháp luật và nhu cầu kiểm soát quyền lực nhà nước ở Việt Nam hiện nay [Constitutional liability in the current context of legal reform and the need for controlling state powers in Vietnam],"* Tạp chí Luật học [Journal of Jurisprudence], (2019) 5, at 75–77.

[19] TRAN Thanh Huong, *Những bảo đảm pháp lý cho việc thực hiện quyền cơ bản của công dân trong lĩnh vực Tự do cá nhân [Legal guarantees of the implementation of basic rights of citizens in terms of individual liberty], Hanoi,* PhD thesis (2006) at 143.

documents or implementing legal documents are effective and have lower legal value in comparison with laws, sometimes, the former seems to be implemented better and have a higher actual value. For instance, in some cases, there are some implementing legal documents have regulations that are contrary to the instructed one.[20] Therefore, future amendments of the Vietnamese Constitution need to clarify the principle of the direct effect of the Constitution in general and, in particular, all constitutional rights should be allowed to have immediate effect. In addition, constitution-makers should, if necessary, sketch transitional provisions that provide a roadmap for implementing constitutional rights.[21]

3. Teaching Constitutional Law in Universities in Ho Chi Minh City

Constitutional Law is a mandatory subject that is categorized into the general knowledge discipline group of the bachelor of laws program offered by legal training institutions in Ho Chi Minh City. The subject is usually taught in a 3-credit course, which is designed to equip students with knowledge on both theoretical and practical legal issues concerning constitutions and their place in the legal system. Consequently, this paper analyzes the teaching and learning of constitutional law in some legal training institutions in Ho Chi Minh City based on two criteria, namely: the subject contents and the teaching method.

3.1 Subject contents

In terms of subject contents, there are two popular models for constitutional law courses offered by legal training institutions in Ho Chi Minh City:

---

[20] NGUYEN Minh Doan, *Thực hiện và áp dụng pháp luật ở Việt Nam [The implementation and application of laws in Vietnam]*, (Hanoi: National Political Publishing, 2009) at 137.

[21] LUU Duc Quang, *supra note 2*, at 110–116.

3.1.1 The first model

The first model is the "traditional" model, which is a long-established model that has been and is still widely applied by training institutions in Ho Chi Minh City, among which the most notable is Ho Chi Minh City University of Law.[22] In this model, apart from the compulsory general knowledge, the other content of the subject is designed to closely follow the titles of the chapters and the structure of the current Constitution. If the Constitution changes, the subject contents also change subsequently; for instance, the change of the name of Chapter 10 in the constitutional law curriculum from "People's Councils and People's Committees" in 2012 to "Local Governments" in 2014 is a reflection of a change in the 2013 Constitution. This model simply reflects the written words of the Constitution and promotes the knowledge of the Constitution of Vietnam. The perceptions and approaches of the students are, as a consequence, usually limited to those of Vietnamese legislators only. This is also a general legal teaching method in Vietnam today.

3.1.2 The second model

The second and newer model is viewed as an innovative one, with the pioneer being the Ho Chi Minh City University of Economics.[23] Currently, the University of Economics and Law also applies this model to teach law, including constitutional law. Under this model, the subject's contents aim to equip learners with fundamental knowledge, including the formation and development of

---

[22] Constitutional Law Syllabus of Ho Chi Minh City University of Law (2018) includes the following topics: (1) Introduction to constitution law and the Constitution of Vietnam; (2) Political regime; (3) Human rights, basic rights and duties of citizens; (4) Overview of state apparatus of the Socialist Republic of Vietnam; (5) Election regime; (6) National Assembly; (7) State President; (8) Government; (9) The People's Court and People's Procuracy; (10) Local government.

[23] Constitutional Law Syllabus of University of Economics Ho Chi Minh City (2019) includes following topics: (1) Introduction to constitutional law; (2) Constitutions; (3) Constitution making; (4) Form of governments; (5) Constitutional institutions; (6) Constitutional rights; (7) Constitutional jurisdiction; (8) Recent trends in development of constitution law.

constitutions, main constitutional topics, approaches in constitutional law, and a general overview of the Constitution. In addition, it places the Vietnamese Constitution in a comparative context. As such, this model covers the common perceptions of mankind about the Constitution and constitutional Law in the context of integration. Therefore, it helps learners enhance their critical and systematic thinking skills and nurture their ability to conduct comparative research on the constitutions of different countries. Moreover, this model also fosters awareness and attitudes of students about respecting constitutional values, including written constitutions, prescriptive constitutions, the rule of law, protection of human rights, decentralization, and constitutional jurisdiction.

3.2 Teaching methods

Methods employed in teaching constitutional law vary depending on many different factors, namely: the educational philosophy of each law training institution, lecturer capacity, the number of students, subject time allocation, and learning materials. Currently, the teaching methodologies of constitutional law in legal training institutions in Ho Chi Minh City vary. This paper focuses on introducing some positive teaching methods such as thematic discussions, case solving, simulation, and role-play. These teaching practices are referenced to the teaching of Constitutional Law at the Ho Chi Minh City University of Law, University of Economics and Law (Vietnam National University - Ho Chi Minh City), University of Economics, Ho Chi Minh City University of Social Sciences and Humanities (Vietnam National University–Ho Chi Minh City), and Saigon University.

3.2.1 Group discussions

Under this teaching method, the lecturer offers topics and students are put into groups to conduct research on the topics from outside the lecture halls/classrooms and later discuss their findings in class under the guidance of the lecturer. Through the discussions, each student gets to understand the legal nature of the topics and draws their own conclusions. Also, students are exposed to different views, and they are equally allowed to express their views. On the other hand, the lecturer is able to observe students' understanding of the topics to make reasonable adjustments to enhance students' ability to analyze, criticize, and solve problems.[24] Some examples of specific topics are as follows:

- **Values of the 1946 Constitution of the Democratic Republic of Vietnam:** The 1946 Constitution was the first Constitution of Vietnam. The constitution-making process, the content, and the constitution implementation process left many precious lessons. Please analyze the inheritance of values of the constitution-making process, the content of the constitution, and its implementation process.

- **Emperor Abdication:** Over the years, kings of many constitutional monarchs have abdicated their authorities (e.g., the Cambodian King, the Queen of the Netherlands, and the Japan Emperor). In reference to specific countries where this has happened, research more about the context of such abdications. How does this behavior affect the constitutional institution of those countries? What do you think about the future of constitutional monarchy in the world?

- **Impeachment:** In 2017, Park Geun-hye, the President of South Korea, was disposed by the constitutional court and later sentenced to imprisonment for corruption and abuse of power. On September 24, 2019, the impeachment investigation of Donald Trump, the 45th president of the United States, was intiated when Nancy Pelosi, the President of the US House of Representatives, declared in a speech on television that there was need to initiate a formal impeachment investigation against President Trump. Research on the impeachment process and the history of impeachment of the presidents in the two countries above. In your opinion, what is the relationship between the impeachment process and the checks and balances mechanism recognized

---

[24] Garry Hess – Steven Friedland, *Phương pháp dạy và học đại học (Từ thực tiễn ngành Luật)*, (Hanoi: Youth Publishing House, 2005) at 36–38.

in the United States and Korean Constitutions? Please refer to the process of handling responsibility for senior officials in Vietnam.

3.2.2 Role-play simulation

This session is simulated as an interrogation session of Ministers in the National Assembly's room. The lecturer divides the class into groups of about five students each. Each group is then tasked with the role of presiding over a questioning session, with the National Assembly deputies being the students who pose questions and the ministers being the students who answer the questions. The simulation questions at the National Assembly's interpellation are required to reflect the current controversial issues in reality; for example, the Minister of Education and Training answers questions regarding the launch of primary school textbooks and their use and the Minister of Natural Resources and Environment answers questions about land allocation and management of land used for religious facilities. These discussions allow students an opportunity to gain experience on the process of questioning and answering questions in parliament, to learn about supreme supervision activities of the National Assembly, and to be able to identify the legal status of National Assembly deputies and ministers.

The use of simulation activities is particularly useful for legal practice and for the development of personal traits such as time management and assertiveness. The role-play aims to achieve three educational goals: cognitive capacity, legal practice skills, and emotional traits when practicing law. Simulation and role-play activities help students strengthen their presentation and debate skills, and they stimulate them to exercise their brains through parliamentary experience. Moreover, such activities allow students an opportunity to apply their knowledge about the supreme power of supervision of the National Assembly over activities of the government and the interpellation sessions conducted by the National Assembly in the classroom as well as enhance and systematize their social knowledge.

3.2.3. Case study method

This method requires students to apply their legal knowledge to identify and resolve legal problems that are presented in the context of real-life experiences in the classroom (real life in class).[25] This allows students an opportunity to practice their legal skills, namely: analytical and interpretive skills, investigative skills, public relations skills, consulting skills, and solving professional and ethical issues based on critical legal thinking.

For example, students were asked to read the case below and answer the subsequent questions as follows:

[Facts]

In the evening of April 1, 2019, Mr. NHL (61-year-old, former Vice Chief Prosecutor of Da Nang and lawyer of Danang Bar Association) was caught hugging and kissing a girl despite her resistance. A building's surveillance camera recorded the incident and the short video obtained from the camera went viral on social networks, consequently, sparking public concerns. Legal experts also started debating whether or not Mr. NHL had committed child sexual abuse. On April 21, 2019, the police in Ho Chi Minh City's District 4 prosecuted the accused for child sexual molestation and he was forbidden from leaving his residence.

On April 24, Mrs. TTTT, the wife of Mr. NHL, filed a denunciation on the grounds of being humiliated. Accordingly, Mrs. TTTT requested the police to investigate entities that sprayed paint and threw dirt into her house and those who used offensive words against her in the media and social networks. According to Article 155 of the Penal Code 2015, these acts amount to humiliation. On April 26, Tan penned a letter to the netizens, stating that the past 25 days have been the toughest time in her life. When sending this letter, her family temporarily left their own house for a while. Mrs. TTTT wished that everyone could share this letter because her family life had been turned upside down and their spirit was

---

[25] Ibid, at 62–63.

crushed. "I hope that the story will end here, you should not commit these offensive activities to me and my children. Our bearable goes beyond our limitations," she wrote. On April 27, Tran Phuoc Huong, the Chief of the Public Security Office in Hai Chau District, confirmed that Mrs. TTTT had withdrawn the letter of denunciation, which had alleged that her family had been "humiliated" without reason.

From the end of April to the beginning of July 2019, a group of parents practicing law in HCM City launched a campaign with the message "Punish pedophiles - Protect Children" and "When a child is being abused, call for 111 (24/7)– A national child protection hotline." After getting media coverage, the campaign caught the attention of many people and supported by tens of thousands of people.

On June 25, 2019, at the first-instance trial, the victim was absent and refused to receive protection from lawyers. The court directed that further investigation was needed. On July 27, 2019, District 4's procuracy again prosecuted NHL for molestation of a person under 16 years old. The accused was handed an 18-month jail term, but he appealed immediately after the ruling.

Resolving the situation. The lecturer will divide students into groups of five students. Each group will play a part in this situation, discuss internally, present, and debate the matters as follows:

[Question 1] Please comment on the people's behavior in order to clarify the manifestations of the rule of law.

[Question 2] You will play a role in the situation to resolve conflicts, including the victim's family; suspects and relatives; the authorities (the investigation agency, procuracy, and the court); residents and apartment management; and other publics.

[Question 3] In your opinion, what measures should the government and general public urgently take to prevent the prevalence of child abuse in general and sexual abuse against children in particular?

3.3 Examination and evaluation

Evaluating students' achievements in Constitutional Law at the University of Economics and Law, the Ho Chi Minh City University of Law, and the University of Economics Ho Chi Minh City mainly relies on their overall performance in mid-term evaluation (accounting for 30% to 50%) and final evaluation (accounting from 50% to 70%). A mid-term evaluation may be conducted using various evaluation methods. For example, students are obliged, in groups or individually, to take tests and students' average test scores then become the mid-term scores or students are divided into small groups (5–7 students per group) to prepare for the assignment given to each group by the lecturer. The students will then present and discuss their assignments in class. The final evaluation may be administered in the following forms: (1) as an oral test or (2) written examinations that have to be completed within an allocated time (often 75–90 minutes). Concerning written examinations, students are allowed to use any document or only normative documents depending on the lecturer.

For instance, the following questions were asked in the final 2019 examinations that were administered to students at the University of Economics and Law. Students were asked to answer them in 75 minutes.

[Question 1] (4 points) - Questions about the state apparatus

1. Please analyze the relationship between the State President and the National Assembly in accordance with current laws.

2. On October 23, 2018, the XIV National Assembly elected Mr. Nguyen Phu Trong as the State President in the term from 2016 to 2021. After this event, some commentators believe that this is the unification of the titles of the General Secretary and the State President in Vietnam. Please give your opinion.

[Question 2] (6 points) - Questions about civil rights

On August 19, 2014, Mr. Do Ngoc Tung, Vice Chairman of the People's Committee of the commune, and Mr. Ly Minh Tu, Deputy Head of the Police Department of Nghia Ho Commune (Luc Ngan District, Bac Giang), confirmed in the record of Mr. Nguyen Van Vung (Nguyen Thi Tinh's younger brother) with the content as follows: "Mrs. Nguyen Thi Tinh, born in 1981, during the time of residing in the locality, she herself and her family did not follow the guidelines and policies of the Party, the laws of the State and local regulations (some donations)." The confirmation resulted in the fact that Mr. Nguyen Van Vung was not eligible to be recruited to the police force.

Mrs. Tinh also acknowledged that in 2013, her family did not contribute to the locality's funds regrading three payments, including the flood and storm prevention fund, defence-security fund, and dioxin fund. However, she stated that the record of the commune officials seriously violated the honor, dignity, and prestige of her husband and her. As mentioned bases, Mrs. Tinh filed a case in court and requested Mr. Ly Minh Tu, Mr. Do Ngoc Tung, the People's Committee, and the Police Department of Nghia Ho to compensate damages relating to infringement on the honor, dignity, and prestige of her husband and her. (Source: Tuoi Tre Newspaper, August 30, 2019)

Please answer these following questions:

[Question 1] Which human rights and civil rights principles regulated in Constitutional Law of 2013 are involved in the situation?

[Question 2] Please comment on the conduct of the related subjects?

[Question 3] From your perspective, what should the government and citizens do to effectively implement the constitutional principles on human rights and civil rights?

Chapter 4

CONSTITUTIONAL RIGHTS WITH SPECIAL REFERENCE TO THE ROLE OF THE EXTRAORDINARY CHAMBERS IN THE COURTS OF CAMBODIA (ECCC)

Meas Bora*

(Cambodian University for Specialties)

1. Introduction

This is a transcript text of my lecture on constitutional rights and their enforcement by the ECCC. This lecture was delivered at the Hanoi Law University on 9 September 2019 as part of the summer course organized and supported by the Keio University of Japan. Following this part, the second part describes the historical development of Cambodian constitutions up to 1993. This part presents more detailed principles and rights espoused in the constitutions to promote awareness of this constitution through teaching and research, the third part of this text illustrates the extent to which constitutional law has been taught in Cambodia. The fourth part presents the actual realization of constitutional rights by the ECCC and the fifth part sums up the whole presentation.

---

* Dr. MEAS Bora graduated from Graduate School of Law of Nagoya University in 2007. Now, he is the president of Cambodian University for Specialties (CUS) and law lecturer (international law, human rights and international criminal justice). He has 12 year work experience with the ECCC, starting from legal official to legal team leader of the Office of the Co-Investigating Judge.

2. Up to the 1993 Constitution

2.1 Cambodian Constitutions

Cambodia is a constitutional monarchy with a parliamentary form of government.[1] Before the 1993 Constitution, five constitutions, starting from the 1947 modeled Constitution of the Fourth French Republic, had been promulgated in Cambodia. The second Constitution was promulgated in 1972 when the Khmer Republic, under the influence of the US political ideologies, created a parliament consisting of the National Assembly and the Senate as well as other principles such as checks and balances.[2] The third Constitution was promulgated during Communist Party (Khmer Rouge) regime after it toppled the Khmer Republic regime.[3] After the 1979 liberation from the Khmer Rouge, the People's Republic of Kampuchea was established and adopted the 1981 Constitution, which is the fourth Constitution in the historical development of Cambodia's constitutions.[4] During the transitional period, the fifth constitution (the 1991 Constitution) was promulgated to aid Cambodia change its regime to the State of Cambodia.[5] Finally, after October 23, 1991 and the 1993 general election, Cambodia promulgated the 1993 Constitution.[6]

2.1.1 Key Principles and Elements in the 1993 Constitution

The 1993 Constitution is of significant and comprehensive compared to the previous constitutions. It contains key principles on sovereignty[7], multi-party and

---

[1] YAN Vandeluxe, the Historical Development of Cambodia's Constitutions *in* Cambodian Constitutional Law, HOR Peng, KONG Phallack, Jorg Menzel *ed.*, 2016, p. 58 (Cambodian Constitutional Law).

[2] *Id.*, p. 60.

[3] *Id.*, p. 61.

[4] *Id.*, p. 62.

[5] Jorg MENZEL, Cambodia from Civil War to a Constitution to Constitutionalism? *in* Cambodian Constitutional Law, p. 15.

[6] YAN Vandeluxe, *supra* note 1, pp. 63–64.

[7] Chapter I of the 1993 Cambodian Constitution.

liberal democracy as reflected in regular universal and direct suffrage elections,[8] separation of powers,[9] independence of judiciary,[10] and constitutional monarchy.[11] The 1993 Constitution established the king regime, a Congress composed of the National Assembly and the Senate,[12] and a Cambodian Constitutional Council (CCC) similar to one of previous constitution.[13]

Guaranteeing the rule of law, democracy, and fundamental human rights in Chapter III (Article 31–50) are positive developments. In addition, there are many provisions on international law elements, including treaties that can be terminated[14] and bodies in charge of signing and ratification of treaties.[15]

Article 31 highlights the relationship between international law and Cambodian laws. This includes the ratification of international treaties or agreements so that they are recognized as part of Cambodian laws. In 2007, the CCC issued one important decision to clarify the provisions of this Article. It said that:

"Understands that at case trial, in principle, a judge shall not only rely on article 8 of the Law on Aggravating Circumstances for Felonies, but also relies on the law. The term "the law" here refers to the national law including the Constitution which is the supreme law and other applicable laws as well as the international conventions that Cambodia has recognized, especially the Convention on the Rights of the Child."

---

[8] Article 1, Chapter I.

[9] Articles Article 51 new, 128 new, 130 new.

[10] Article 128 new.

[11] Articles 1, 10, 153 new.

[12] Chapters VII and VIII.

[13] Chapter XII.

[14] Article 55.

[15] Articles 26 new.

3. Teaching Constitutional Law

After the 1993 elections, free economic market and privatization policies were implemented in the field of education. As a result, in addition to state institutions, many private schools and universities were created and recognized by the Royal Government of Cambodia[16] to provide training at all levels.

In Cambodia, constitutional law is taught at both general and higher education levels. At the general education level, from Grade 1 to 12, constitutional law is not taught as a subject; only its key principles or content related to issues worth of informing pupils are taught. In specific, human rights, equality, and election rights are part of Grade 1 through Grade 6 instructions and Civic Studies, which also touches on constitutional rights, is taught from Grade 7 to 9. Similar to other fields, a teacher-centered approach is used in teaching *Moral and Civic Study*.[17]

At the higher education level, constitutional law is taught as a compulsory subject during the foundation year of study and the first year of an associate's and bachelor's degree in law.[18] Besides, constitutional issues and principles are further emphasized during criminal law, human rights, introduction to law, institutions study, and international law classes. For example, when discussing about the place of international law in the Cambodian legal system, Article 31 of the 1993 Constitution is referred.

Constitutional law is taught for 45–48 hours within a period of three to six months, depending on the mode of study (i.e., regular or part-time). Weekend classes last for three hours. After attendance and passing the final exam as well as others assignments or class activities administered by each individual lecturer, students get three credits for this unit. The teaching method employed in teaching constitutional law is a mixture of teacher-centered approach and student centered approach. However, the latter is much more common than the

---

[16] SOTH Sang Bonn, Teaching Constitutional law, the Historical Development of Cambodia's Constitutions *in* Cambodian Constitutional Law, p. 95.

[17] *Id.*, pp. 93, 95.

[18] *Id.*, p. 97.

former. Students listen to lectures by professors, accompanied by discussions or presentations. There are also study tours to public institutions[19] such as the CCC. Judgments or decisions are rarely used or referred to during lectures, although they are available online.[20]

4. The Role of ECCC in Enforcing Constitutional Rights

4.1 Constitutional Rights

There are many types of rights guaranteed under the 1993 Constitution, key among them being political rights[21], social rights[22], economic rights[23], civil rights[24] and more specifically rights of children and women[25]. Articles 32 and 38 provide more details about the right to personal liberty, the right to life and the right to criminal justice.

4.2 The Enforcement of Rights by ECCC

4.2.1 ECCC

ECCC is a mixed court that was established by the Agreement between the United Nations and the Royal Government of Cambodia Concerning the Prosecution under Cambodian Law of Crimes Committed during the Period of Democratic Kampuchea to respond to bring to trial senior leaders and those who were responsible for crimes and violations of Cambodian law during the regime of Democratic Kampuchea. Article 1 of the Agreement stipulates that: *The purpose of this law is to bring to trial senior leaders of Democratic Kampuchea and*

---

[19] *Id.*, p. 102.
[20] Decisions at https://www.ccc.gov.kh/index_en.php#about
[21] Article 34 new, 1993 Constitution.
[22] Article 43.
[23] Article 36.
[24] Article 45.
[25] Article 46.

those who were most responsible for the crimes and serious violations of Cambodian penal law, international humanitarian law and custom, and international conventions recognized by Cambodia, that were committed during the period from 17 April 1975 to 6 January 1979.

Besides this Agreement and the law on ECCC, there are also internal rules enacted to deal with procedural issues. The rights of accused persons are provided in international instruments, such as the International Covenant on Civil and Political Rights to which Cambodia joined.[26] The maximum sentence for crimes in the ECCC Law is life imprisonment.

4.2.2 The Right to Life

Article 32 of the Constitution does not allow the death penalty. It stipulates that: *"Everybody shall have the rights to life, freedom, and personal security. Capital punishment is prohibited."* There have been two instances in which the ECCC has enforced this provision. First, based on the principle of legality, as read together with Article 1 of ECCC (quoted above), the applicable laws, either written or customary law, shall be in force before the commission of a crime—they should not operate retrospectively. The maximum sentence applied to national crimes in the Criminal Code of Cambodia in 1956 was the death penalty. However, the provision on the death penalty in the drafted law on ECCC law was held to be unconstitutional by the CCC.[27] Finally, given that the court has to observe the rights of accused persons, they are entitled to appropriate imprisonment terms. For instance, in case 001, the Trial Chamber of the ECCC issued a lower sentence to the accused. This triggered reactions from civil society and victims.

---

[26] Cambodia signed 1980 and ratified 1992, https://treaties.un.org/Pages/ViewDetails.aspx?src= TREATY& mtdsg_no=IV-4&chapter=4&clang=_en

[27] Decision of the Constitutional Council 040/002/2001 KBDH.C of 12 February 2001.

4.2.3 Right to Personal Liberty

Article 38 of the 1993 Constitution prohibits all physical abuse of any individual. The Constitution protects the life, honor, and dignity of its citizens. The ECCC law and internal rules do not have such provisions; however, there are provisions that accused persons can invoke to ensure that their lives are respected and protected. For instance, Internal Rule 21 provides a broad remedial mechanism in addition to the right to appeal.[28] Below is a case scenario illustrating how the ECCC chambers observe the accused persons' rights.

Duch was a middle rank cadre of the Democratic Kampuchea Regime. He was the chief of a central prison named S21. He was arrested and detained by the Cambodian Military Court during the drafting of the ECCC Agreement. There were a number of military court decisions on prosecuting crimes similar to the ones under discussion in the drafted Agreement.[29] In addition, there were laws on provisional detention, extending detention to three years for charged crimes and a period longer than three years for national crimes.[30] This triggered a request to review the constitutionality of the law, and the CCC was of the view that the law was constitutional.[31]

Duch's right to personal liberty was raised from the beginning of the proceedings. He argued that the pre-trial detention violated his right to personal liberty and that it amounted to an abuse of process, asserting that his illegal detention in military court facility was meant to bar the ECCC from determining his case and finally releasing him.[32] During adversary proceedings, while accepting the doctrine of abuse of process, the Co-Investigating Judges (CIJs) found no serious violations of *Duch's* rights, such as the right to freedom from torture, and

---

[28] Internal Rules of ECCC, *see* https://www.eccc.gov.kh/en/document/legal/internal-rules

[29] ECCC, Trial Chamber, Decision on Request for Release, E39/5 (public), 15 June 2009, para. 2.

[30] CCC, Decision No. 13, 25 August 1999, p. 1.

[31] *Id.*

[32] ECCC, Co-Investigating Judges, Order of Provisional Detention, C3/10, 31 July 2007, para. 4.

based on international jurisprudence and the gravity of the crimes he was alleged to have committed, decided that the ECCC was not barred by this doctrine and pursued to detain him.[33] *Duch* filed an appeal against the Provisional Detention Order to the Pre-Trial Chamber. The Chamber ruled that it has no jurisdiction to examine whether detention by a military court is illegal.[34] However, the Chamber considered whether the grounds upon which the CIJs ordered *Duch's* continued detention were justified.[35] It reaffirmed those grounds.[36]

Finally, during trial by the Trial Chamber (TC), *Duch* based his preliminary objection on illegal detention and requested for his release.[37] The TC examined the facts of the case and found that the detention was illegal. It then went ahead to give a landmark decision, which is fully quoted below:

"FINDS that the detention of the Accused by the Military Court was an error of application of procedural law, a violation of his rights, and that therefore the detention was unlawful;

DECLARES that the Accused, under international law and the law of the Kingdom of Cambodia, is entitled to a remedy for the time spent in detention under the authority of the Military Court and the violation of his rights;

NOTES that the Accused, in the event of acquittal, may seek appropriate remedies for time spent in detention at the Military Court and for the violation of his rights before the national courts of Cambodia;

DECLARES that, in the event of conviction before the ECCC, and applying Article 503 of the Cambodian Code of Criminal Procedure, the Accused is entitled to credit for the time served in detention under the authority of the ECCC, namely since 31 July 2007;

---

[33] *Id.*, para. 21.

[34] ECCC, Pre-Trial Chamber, Decision on Appeal against Provisional Detention Order of Kaing Guek Eav alias Duch, C5/45, 3 December 2007, para. 25.

[35] *Id.*, para. 41.

[36] *Id.*, part of Conclusion and Orders.

[37] ECCC, Trial Chamber, *supra* note 29, para. 1.

DECLARES further that, in the event of conviction before the ECCC, the Accused is entitled to the remedy of credit for the time spent in detention under the authority of the Military Court, namely from 10 May 1999 to 30 July 2007."

Based on this decision, the TC reduced the imprisonment term for *Duch* by seven years as a remedy for illegal detention.[38] Civil parties and co-prosecutors appealed against this ruling to the Supreme Court Chamber. The Chamber pronounced life imprisonment for *Duch*. It is important to note that the Supreme Court Chamber did support the human rights remedy issued to *Duch* by the TC but the crimes he had committed were more severe, demanding the highest sentence.[39]

Full realization of rights: rights are provided widely in international instruments.[40] State parties, based on various reasons, voluntarily accept those rights by becoming member states to those treaties and ratifying them.

The intention of the international community is to allow full realization of the rights provided for in international instruments. This is expressed in the International Covenant on Civil and Political Rights.[41] There are no indicted measures imposed on States to enforce human rights domestically. A State's choice to honor specific rights depends on its laws, legal mechanisms, and legal systems.[42]

States might take various measures individually or jointly. Three measures are common: First is legislative measures that are meant to revise laws to make

---

[38] *Id.*, p. 15.

[39] ECCC, Supreme Court Chamber, Judgement, F28 (public), 3 February 2012.

[40] For example the International Covenant on Civil and Political Rights (ICCPR), see UN General Assembly, *International Covenant on Civil and Political Rights*, 16 December 1966, United Nations, Treaty Series, vol. 999, p. 171, available at: https://www.refworld.org/docid/3ae6b3aa0.html [accessed 31 October 2019]

[41] *Id.*, Articles 1 and 2.

[42] UN Human Rights Committee, General Comment No. 31 on the Nature of the General Legal Obligation Imposed on States Parties to the Covenant, CCPR/C/21/Rev.1/Add.13, 29 March 2004, para. 7.

them consistent with international treaties. Second is enacting laws required to implement human rights treaties. The law making process is much more demanding for civil law States that adhere to the principle of legality. Laws are not enough and unavoidable to construct by judiciary. Third, the enforcement of human rights depends on the goodwill of the government. If the court renders the correct judgment but the government fails to enforce it, then the full realization of the right in question is obstructed. This is not consistent with the pronouncement that human rights remedies are practical and effective.[43] Therefore, all organs of the State need to work together to ensure full realization of human rights. If one organ fails—for example, the legislature fails to adopt the laws required to pave way for courts to observe human rights—the State as a whole is held to be internationally responsible.[44]

It is clear that *Duch's* right to personal liberty was violated, and he was entitled to a remedy despite the fact that State authorities were the violators of the said rights. The pronouncement of reduction of sentence is a real and practical remedy. Rights are not only on paper; they shall be ensured even those of offenders. If their rights are violated, they must get a remedy.

The decision in *Duch* is priceless. It illustrates how human rights are practically and domestically applied, starting from invocation by alleged victim, then the court examining the facts of the alleged violation, and finally, the court pronouncing a concrete remedy where violations are established. In such scenarios, the court does not only rely on the fact that the State is a party to the relevant treaties, but the submissions of defending lawyers also influence the sentence pronounced. In addition, the court also considers other available remedies in the given circumstances.

---

[43] ICCPR, *supra* note 40, Article 2.

[44] UN Human Rights Committee, General Comment No. 31, *supra* note 42, para. 4.

5. Summary

The 1993 Constitution of Cambodia provides many principles of constitutionalism, including the protection of human rights as mentioned in Article
31. However, these rights have not been fully realized. The ECCC has done a
remarkable job in facilitating the protection of some of these rights, such as the
right to personal liberty, through its landmark jurisprudence confirming effective
remedies for violation of rights, even the ones of accused persons. This should
also be emulated by the national courts of Cambodia.

Chapter 5

PROTECTION OF FUNDAMENTAL RIGHTS IN THE CONSTITUTION OF THE KINGDOM OF THAILAND (B.E. 2560)*

Noppadon Detsomboonrut**

(Thammasat University)

Introduction

Not only do constitutions serve as the supreme law of states and the source of validity of other legal rules in a legal system, they also determine the structures of states as well as political systems and governmental forms of the societies they govern. Apart from their structural significance, based on the concept of constitutionalism, the rule of law, the legal state (Rechtsstaat), and democracy, constitutions are tasked with an ultimate mission, which is to protect the fundamental rights of people. Accordingly, constitutions and constitutional law are an area that is of fundamental importance to legal studies in any jurisprudence. This

---

* This article is based on the lecture given in Keio University Law School and Hanoi Law University Summer School 2019 during November 9–13, 2019 in Hanoi as part of Program for Asian Global Legal Professions (PAGLEP). If not specified otherwise, the English text of the Constitution of the Kingdom of Thailand (B.E. 2560) employed in this article is the unofficial translation by Legal Opinion and Translation Section, Foreign Law Division, the Office of the Council of State.

** Assistant Professor, Faculty of Law, Thammasat University; LLB, Chulalongorn University; LLM, Thammasat University; LLM, University of Cambridge; PhD in Law, University of Edinburgh.

article aims to elaborate the protection of fundamental rights within the Constitution of the Kingdom of Thailand as part of a comparative study of constitutional law and teaching methods focusing on the protection of fundamental rights, which is the overall theme of this book. To achieve this objective, this article is divided into the following three parts: I. Characteristics of the Thai Constitution; II. Constitutional Law Teaching Methods in Thailand: A Case Study of the Faculty of Law, Thammasat University; and III. The Recognition and Protection of Fundamental Rights in the Constitution of the Kingdom of Thailand.

1. Characteristics of the Thai Constitution

The political and social backgrounds to the creation of the current Constitution of Thailand serves as a good starting point to this section because it potentially provides a foundation for understanding the rationale underlying the Constitution as well as the contents of its provisions. On May 20, 2014, the National Council for Peace and Order (hereinafter as the NCPO), led by General Prayuth Chan-ocha, embarked on a coup d'état, seizing power from the caretaker government of Yingluck Shinawatr. The NCPO discarded the 2007 Constitution of the Kingdom of Thailand and established the 2014 Interim Constitution with Sections 32–39 on the new constitution-making process. Section 32 establishes a body called the Constitution Drafting Commission which had the duty and power to propose a new constitution. On March 29, 2016, the Constitution Drafting Commission unveiled the draft of a new constitution. Consequently, a referendum to approve the draft of the new constitution was held on August 8, 2016 and the vote was in favour of it; however, certain provisions of the draft constitution were altered after the referendum.[1] On April 6, 2017, the Constitution of the

---

[1] The sections which were altered are Sections 5, 12, 15, 16 17, 19 and 182. Please note that Section 272 was also altered; however, this was owing to the result of the question that was part of the referendum.

Kingdom of Thailand (B.E. 2560/AD 2017) entered into force.

In terms of its constitutional structure, Thailand adopts a written-constitution system. Accordingly, constitutional rules mainly derive from written provisions of the constitution; however, if there exists any lacuna in those written provisions, Section 5 of the Constitution provides a gap-filling method by which relevant officials, including judges in the Constitutional Court, shall apply "customary constitutional rules" or , to use the wording in the constitution, "the governmental custom of Thailand under the democratic regime with the King as Head of State"[2]to fill the gaps of the written provisions of the constitution. Based on the text of Section 3 and the written-constitution approach, customary constitutional law may be resorted to and applied to a case if and only if there are no written provisions of the Constitution applicable to relevant cases.[3] Therefore, customary constitutional law shall not be applied in a manner that is incompati-

---

[2] Paragraph 2 of Section 5 provides: "Whenever no provision under this Constitution is applicable to a case, an act shall be performed or a decision shall be made in accordance with the governmental custom of Thailand under the democratic regime of government with the King as Head of State." (In certain translations, e.g., the unofficial translation by the Office of the Council of State, the word "convention" is employed instead of governmental custom. However, as the notion of "constitutional conventions", which exist in certain legal systems that adopt an unwritten constitutional approach, is incompatible with the content of Paragraph 2 of Section 5, as constitutional conventions can alter the consequence of written constitutional rules in practice. However, customary constitutional rules or to use the wording in the constitution, "the governmental custom of Thailand" cannot be applied in a fashion incompatible with the written rules of the Constitution. Thus, as the use of the term convention is potentially misleading, the author opts not to employ the term "convention" as the translation of "ประเพณีการปกครองประเทศไทย". Please see more on constitutional conventions in, e.g., Albert Venn Dicey, *Introduction to the Study of the Law of the Constitution* (Liberty Classics 1939); Anthony W Bradley, Keith D Ewing and Christopher JS Knight, *Constitutional and Administrative Law* (16th edn, Pearson 2015).

[3] Please see The Constitution Drafting Commission, *Purposes and Section by Section Commentary on the Constitution of the Kingdom of Thailand B.E. 2560* (ความมุ่งหมายและคำอธิบายประกอบรายมาตรา ของรัฐธรรมนูญแห่งราชอาณาจักรไทย พุทธศักราช ๒๕๖๐) (2562) 7. <https:// cdc.parliament.go.th/draftconstitution2/ewt_dl_link.php?nid=1042&filename=index> accessed 23 October 2019.

ble with the written rules of the Constitution. The Constitution adopts a democracy as the political system of Thailand, with the King as Head of State[4] and a parliamentary system as the form of government.[5] The National Assembly consists of two houses: the House of Representatives and the Senate. While members of the former are elected on either a constituency basis or a party-list basis,[6] members of the latter are appointed by the King upon the advice of the NCPO during the transition period[7] and, after that, a self-selection process is conducted to select eligible candidates in each specified field of expertise.[8]

Regarding constitutional amendments, the constitutional amendment process of the current constitution makes it relatively difficult to amend, compared to the past Thai Constitutions. Article 255, which acts as an eternity clause, prohibits changing the democratic regime of government with the King as Head of State or changing the form of the state.[9] According to Section 256,[10] amendments for matters not protected by Section 255 shall be considered in three readings. In the first reading for adoption of principle, an amendment shall be approved by a majority of the total number of existing members of the House of Representatives and the Senate, provided that at least one-third of the existing members of the Senate vote in the affirmative.[11] The second reading for section-by-section consideration simply requires a majority vote of the total number of existing members of both houses.[12] In the third and final reading, the proposal for an amendment must be approved by a majority vote, provided that not less than one-third of the Senate and not less than one-fifth of the total number of members of all political parties whose members do not hold positions as ministers, president or

---

[4] Sections 2 of the Constitution of the Kingdom of Thailand (B.E. 2560).

[5] Section 3 of the Constitution of the Kingdom of Thailand (B.E. 2560).

[6] Section 83 of the Constitution of the Kingdom of Thailand (B.E. 2560).

[7] Section 269 of the Constitution of the Kingdom of Thailand (B.E. 2560).

[8] Section 107 of the Constitution of the Kingdom of Thailand (B.E. 2560).

[9] Section 255 of the Constitution of the Kingdom of Thailand (B.E. 2560).

[10] Section 256 of the Constitution of the Kingdom of Thailand (B.E. 2560).

[11] Section 256 (3) of the Constitution of the Kingdom of Thailand (B.E. 2560).

[12] Section 256 (4) of the Constitution of the Kingdom of Thailand (B.E. 2560).

vice-president of the House of Representatives.[13] Additionally, in a case where an amendment relates to general provisions, the King, the provisions regarding the amendment to the constitution, the qualifications and prohibitions of office-holders under the constitution or the duties or powers of the courts or independent organs, or in a case where an amendment might hinder the courts or independent organs from delivering their mission within scope of their duties or powers, such an amendment must be approved through a referendum.[14]

One of the distinguished characteristics of the current Constitution of Thailand is the exceptional role and power of the Senate. Apart from its special role in approving constitutional amendments discussed in the preceding part, the Senate possesses the power to approve the nomination of judges in the Constitutional Court.[15] Besides, the Senate plays as a key organ in the process of nominating office-holders for independent organs, namely, Ombudsmen,[16] the National Anti-Corruption Commission,[17] the State Audit Commission[18] and the National Human Rights Commission.[19] Also, during a transition period —the period of five years from the date of installation of the first National Assembly under this constitution— the Senate, together with the House of Representative, has the power to approve the appointment of the Prime Minister.[20] The significance of the role and power of the Senate has been an issue of concern, given the lack of democratic legitimacy in the selection process for members of the Senate, especially during the transition period during which members of the Senate are appointed by the King upon the advice of the NCPO.[21]

---

[13] Section 256 (6) of the Constitution of the Kingdom of Thailand (B.E. 2560).

[14] Section 256 (8) of the Constitution of the Kingdom of Thailand (B.E. 2560).

[15] Section 204 of the Constitution of the Kingdom of Thailand (B.E. 2560).

[16] Section 228 of the Constitution of the Kingdom of Thailand (B.E. 2560).

[17] Section 232 of the Constitution of the Kingdom of Thailand (B.E. 2560).

[18] Section 238 of the Constitution of the Kingdom of Thailand (B.E. 2560).

[19] Section 246 of the Constitution of the Kingdom of Thailand (B.E. 2560).

[20] Section 272 of the Constitution of the Kingdom of Thailand (B.E. 2560).

[21] Section 269 of the Constitution of the Kingdom of Thailand (B.E. 2560).

2. Constitutional Law Teaching Methods in Thailand: A Case Study of the Faculty of Law, Thammasat University

Before discussing the methods used in teaching constitutional law, let this part begin with one intriguing effect of the Thai political reality on academic development. The frequent discarding and creation of constitutions throughout the history of Thailand inevitably affects the study and teaching methods of constitutional law in Thailand. Obviously, the number of textbooks which provide elaborations or discussions based on a section-by-section basis is very limited.[22] Besides the frequent changes, the fact that the interim constitutions created and enforced during periods of military government have a tendency not to be in conformity with the principles entailed in the concepts of democracy, liberalism, constitutionalism, a legal state or the rule of law is another factor that contributes to this situation.

The methods for teaching constitutional law employed in the Faculty of Law, Thammasat University include a doctrinal approach, a theoretical approach, a philosophical approach, a comparative approach and a socio-historical approach. The creation of understanding and critical analyses of textual contents based on the doctrinal study of constitutional rules together with relevant case-law as an elaboration of provisions serves as a basic foundation teaching method for constitutional law classes. Nevertheless, doctrinal study is pursued together with the creation of understanding of relevant philosophies, theories and political, social and historical contexts. The discussion of relevant theories, such as social contracts, constituent power theory, the legal state, the rule of law, democracy, liberalism and Marxism as well as more philosophical concepts such as Kelsen's grundnorm (i.e., basic norm) and H.L.A. Hart's rule of recognition, to name but a few examples, are included in the teaching to provide theoretical guidelines for

---

[22] An example of rare textbooks to provide an elaboration on a section-by-section basis is Yud Saeng-uthai, *The Constitution of The Kingdom of Thailand (B.E.) Section by Section Commentary and Short General Commentary on The Constitution (คำอธิบายรัฐธรรมนูญ พ.ศ. 2511 (เรียงมาตรา) และคำอธิบายรัฐธรรมนูญทั่วไปโดยย่อ* (Krung Siam Kan Pim 1968).

understanding and criticizing the content of the constitutions. In addition, given the uniqueness of Thai politics with 20 constitutions within its less than 100 years of its constitutional history since its first constitution, each constitution and its differences from other constitutions cannot be clearly comprehended without studying the social and political contexts of the time of each constitution. Moreover, the study of the whole constitutional history and other relevant events[23] also provides a clear picture of the ongoing problems rooted in Thai society behind the political crises and the lackluster status of Thai constitutions as the supreme law of the land. A comparative law approach is also employed as a teaching method, especially where the sections in question are modeled based on particular foreign constitutional law.

The teaching style mostly depends on the size of the class. Whereas, due to the large number of students per class (around 100–200 students) in a bachelor degree program, constitutional law classes tend to be taught in a lecture-based style, classes for master's students tend to be conducted in a seminar style because of the small number of students per class (around 20–30 students).

3. Recognition and Protection of Fundamental Rights in the Constitution of the Kingdom of Thailand

In its Preamble, the Constitution of the Kingdom of Thailand stipulates that reform and strengthening of the governance of Thailand can be carried out by, *inter alia*:

...guaranteeing, safeguarding and protecting Thai people's rights and liberties more clearly and inclusively by recognising that the Thai people's rights

---

[23] Please see Thai constitutional History in Andrew Harding and Peter Leyland, *The Constitutional System of Thailand: A Contextual Analysis* (Hart Publishing 2011); and Supoj Dantrakul, *Constitutional History (ประวัติรัฐธรรมนูญ)* (Social Science Institute 2550).

and liberties are the principle, while the restriction and limitation thereon are exceptions, provided that the exercise of such rights and liberties must be subject to the rules for protecting the public; prescribing the duties of the State towards people, as well as requiring the people to have duties towards the State...[24]

Also, in Chapter I of the Constitution, "General Provisions", Section 4 states: "Human dignity, rights, liberties and equality of the people shall be protected. The Thai people shall enjoy equal protection under the Constitution." According to the Preamble and Section 4, the equal protection of human dignity, rights, liberties and equality is the main purpose of the Constitution. Therefore, the interpretation of other provisions of the Constitution and other rules of the Thai legal system is bound to be compatible with the Preamble and Section 4 in light of its teleological and systemic interpretation.

In Chapter III of the Constitution, "Rights and Liberties of The Thai People", Sections 25–27 lay down the general rules for the protection of fundamental rights while Sections 28–48 provide for the protection of specific fundamental rights and liberties.

Paragraph I of Section 25[25] sets out a general protection clause of fundamental rights. It provides that, in addition to the rights and liberties specifically guaranteed by the Constitution, the Thai people shall also enjoy "the rights and liberties to perform any act which is not prohibited or restricted by the Constitution or other laws". Although, this provision in itself does not set any require-

---

[24] The Preamble of the Constitution of the Kingdom of Thailand (B.E. 2560).

[25] Paragraph 1 of Section 25 of the Constitution of the Kingdom of Thailand (B.E. 2560) states: "As regards the rights and liberties of the Thai people, in addition to the rights and liberties as guaranteed specifically by the provisions of the Constitution, a person shall enjoy the rights and liberties to perform any act which is not prohibited or restricted by the Constitution or other laws, and shall be protected by the Constitution, insofar as the exercise of such rights or liberties does not affect or endanger the security of the State or public order or good morals, and does not violate the rights or liberties of other persons."

ment on "other laws" that create restrictive effects on those fundamental rights and liberties not specifically recognized by the constitution, the requirements for the enactment of laws which have a restrictive effect on fundamental rights laid down in Section 26, which will be discussed later, shall be applied. Paragraph 1 of Section 25 also provides that the scope of the exercise of fundamental rights and liberties not specifically recognized shall be "insofar as the exercise of such rights or liberties does not affect or endanger the security of the State or public order or good morals, and does not violate the rights or liberties of other persons." Such the scope of the exercise of rights and liberties not specifically recognized by the Constitution which is fraught with vagueness, creating a high level of uncertainty, has a potential to devalue this general protection clause as a tool to promote and protect fundamental rights.

Paragraph 2 of Section 25 establishes a rule of immediate effect of constitutional rights without the need to have a law to elaborate the scope and content of those rights. Nevertheless, such constitutional rights shall be in accordance with the spirit of the Constitution[26] Further, Paragraphs 3 and 4 guarantee the right to access to justice and the right to remedies and legal aid, respectively, in cases of violations of constitutional rights.[27]

Section 26 lays down the requirements for the enactment of laws which have a restrictive effect on fundamental rights. Although the protection of fundamental rights and liberties is the ultimate aim of democracy, the rule of law, the legal

---

[26] Paragraph 2 of Section 25 of the Constitution of the Kingdom of Thailand states: "Any right or liberty stipulated by the Constitution to be as provided by law, or to be in accordance with the rules and procedures prescribed by law, can be exercised by a person or community, despite the absence of such law, in accordance with the spirit of the Constitution."

[27] Paragraphs 3 and 4 of Section 25 the Constitution of the Kingdom of Thailand states:

"Any person whose rights or liberties protected under the Constitution are violated, can invoke the provisions of the Constitution to exercise his or her right to bring a lawsuit or to defend himself or herself in the Court.

Any person injured from the violation of his or her rights or liberties or from the commission of a criminal offence by another person, shall have the right to remedy or assistance from the State, as prescribed by law."

state, as well as constitutionalism, unlimited rights and liberties are equivalent to unlimited violations of rights and liberties. Thus, in a democratic state, a parliament, which receives its mandate from the people via an election, has the legitimate power to enact laws to restrict the constitutional rights and liberties of the people. However, likewise, such a power of parliament is not limitless and the exercise of such power must meet certain conditions. In the case of the Constitution of Thailand, Section 26 governs how the National Assembly shall enact laws restricting constitutional rights[28]. In cases where there exists a specific section articulating the conditions of how to enact laws to restrict a specific constitutional right, the National Assembly law must conform with those conditions. However, in cases where the Constitution does not provide the conditions therein, the laws enacted by the National Assembly must be in conformity with the rule of law, the principle of proportionality and the principle of equality. Further, the justification and necessity for the restriction of the rights and liberties shall also be specified. Nevertheless, according to this constitution, certain fundamental rights cannot be restricted at all, even by virtue of laws enacted by the National Assembly. Such absolute rights which cannot be restricted by law are the right against torture, brutal acts or punishment by cruel or inhumane means,[29] the right of Thai nationals against deportation or prohibition from entering the Kingdom[30] and the

---

[28] Section 26 of the Constitution of the Kingdom of Thailand states:

"The enactment of a law resulting in the restriction of rights or liberties of a person shall be in accordance with the conditions provided by the Constitution.

In the case where the Constitution does not provide the conditions thereon, such law shall not be contrary to the rule of law, shall not unreasonably impose burden on or restrict the rights or liberties of a person and shall not affect the human dignity of a person, and the justification and necessity for the restriction of the rights and liberties shall also be specified.

The law under paragraph one shall be of general application, and shall not be intended to apply to any particular case or person."

[29] Paragraph 4 of Section 28 of the Constitution of Kingdom of Thailand (B.E. 2560) states: "Torture, brutal acts or punishment by cruel or inhumane means shall not be permitted."

[30] Paragraph 1 of Section 39 of the Constitution of the Kingdom of Thailand (B.E. 2560) states: "No person of Thai nationality shall be deported or prohibited from entering the Kingdom."

right of Thai nationals who acquire Thai nationality by birth against revocation of their Thai nationality.[31]

The principle of equal protection of fundamental rights is enshrined in Section 27[32], which embraces the concepts of both formal equality and substantive equality. Paragraph 3 of this section, based on the concept of substantive equality, provides that measures aiming to eliminate an obstacle to or to promote a person's ability to exercise their rights or liberties on the same basis as other persons or to protect or facilitate disadvantaged people, such as children, women, the elderly or persons with disabilities, shall not be deemed unjust discrimination.

Regarding the protection of specific fundamental rights and liberties, Sections 28–48 entail the protection of specific fundamental rights and liberties as follows:

- Section 29: Principle of Non-retroactivity, Presumption of Innocence and the Right against Self-incrimination
- Section 30: Right against Forced Labour
- Section 31: Freedom of Religion

---

[31] Paragraph 2 of Section 39 of the Constitution of the Kingdom of Thailand (B.E. 2560) states: "The revocation of Thai nationality acquired by birth shall not be permitted."

[32] Section 27 of the Constitution of the Kingdom of Thailand (B.E. 2560) states:

"All persons are equal before the law, and shall have rights and liberties and be protected equally under the law.

Men and women shall enjoy equal rights.

Unjust discrimination against a person on the grounds of differences in origin, race, language, sex, age, disability, physical or health condition, personal status, economic and social standing, religious belief, education, or political view which is not contrary to the provisions of the Constitution or on any other grounds, shall not be permitted.

Measures determined by the State in order to eliminate an obstacle to or to promote a person's ability to exercise their rights or liberties on the same basis as other persons or to protect or facilitate children, women, the elderly, persons with disabilities or underprivileged persons shall not be deemed unjust discrimination under paragraph three.

Members of the armed forces, the police force, government officials, other officials of the State, and officers or employees of State organisations shall enjoy the same rights and liberties as those enjoyed by other persons, except those restricted by law specifically in relation to politics, capacities, disciplines or ethics."

- Section 32: Right to Privacy, Right to Dignity, Right to Reputation and Right to Family
- Section 33: Freedom of Dwelling and Right against a Search in a Dwelling or Private Place without a Search Warrant or without other Legal Grounds as provided by law
- Section 34: Freedom of Expression and Academic Freedom
- Section 35: Freedom of the Press
- Section 36: Freedom of Communication
- Section 37: Right to Private Property and Succession
- Section 38: Freedom of Traveling and Freedom of Making the Choice of One's residence
- Section 39: Right of Thai Nationals against Deportation and Prohibition on Entering the Kingdom and Right of Thai Nationals acquiring Thai Nationality by Birth against Revocation of Nationality.[33]
- Section 40: Freedom of Occupation
- Section 41: Right of Individuals and Community to Public Information, Right of Individuals and Community to Make a Petition to the State and Right to Access of Justice in the Case of Violations by the State, State Officers and State's Employees.
- Section 42: Freedom of Association
- Section 43: Cultural, Environmental and Economic Rights of Individuals and

---

[33] Section 49 of the Constitution of the Kingdom of Thailand (B.E. 2560) states:

"No person shall exercise the rights or liberties to overthrow the democratic regime of government with the King as Head of State.

Any person who has knowledge of an act under paragraph one shall have the right to petition the Attorney-General to submit a motion to the Constitutional Court for an order to cease such act.

In case where the Attorney-General orders a refusal to proceed as petitioned or fails to proceed within fifteen days as from the date of receiving the petition, the person making the petition may submit the petition directly to the Constitutional Court.

The action under this section shall not prejudice the criminal prosecution against the person committing an act under paragraph one."

Communities

- Section 44: Freedom of Peaceful Assembly
- Section 45: Freedom to Form a Political Party
- Section 46: Consumer Rights
- Section 47 Right to Public Health Services
- Section 48 Mothers' Pregnancy Rights and the Elderly's Rights

Section 49 which is the last section of Chapter III on "Rights and Liberties of the Thai People", stipulates the scope of the constitutional rights guaranteed by this Constitution. It provides that no person shall exercise constitutional rights or liberties to overthrow the democratic regime of government with the King as Head of State and empowers the Constitutional Court to cease an action not in conformity with this prohibition.[34]

Apart from Chapter III of the Constitution on the "Rights and Liberties of the Thai People", Chapter IV establishes "the Duties of the State. This chapter entails duties of the state to, among others, promote social, economic and cultural benefits of the citizens, such as to provide free compulsory education,[35] efficient universal public health services,[36] basic public utility services with reasonable fees,[37] to maintain and promote cultural ways of life of people and communi-

---

[34] Section 49 of the Constitution of the Kingdom of Thailand (B.E. 2560) provides:

"No person shall exercise the rights or liberties to overthrow the democratic regime of government with the King as Head of State.

Any person who has knowledge of an act under paragraph one shall have the right to petition to the Attorney-General to submit a motion to the Constitutional Court for an order to cease such act.

In the case where the Attorney-General orders a refusal to proceed as petitioned or fails to proceed within fifteen days as from the date of receiving the petition, the person making the petition may submit the petition directly to the Constitutional Court.

The action under this section shall not prejudice the criminal prosecution against the person committing an act under paragraph one."

[35] Section 54 of the Constitution of the Kingdom of Thailand (B.E. 2560).

[36] Section 55 of the Constitution of the Kingdom of Thailand (B.E. 2560).

[37] Section 56 of the Constitution of the Kingdom of Thailand (B.E. 2560).

ties[38] and to conserve and maintain environmental standards, to name but a few examples.[39] Although these duties potentially reflect the correlative rights of the people, the sections regarding the duties of the state are arguably problematic regarding their justiciability because of their nature, which is debatably perceived as more of public policy rather than legal obligations. Even in instances where these duties of state sections are interpreted as creating social and economic rights for the Thai people, the justiciability of social and economic rights is still questionable.[40]

With regard to the constitutional organs for the protection of fundamental rights in the Constitution of the Kingdom of Thailand, the Constitutional Court, the Administrative Courts, the Ombudsman and the National Human Rights Commission are among the organs established by the Constitution and granted the powers and duties relevant to the protection of fundamental rights.[41]

The Constitutional Court has the power to review the constitutionality of bills of law during the law-making process and of laws that are already in force.[42] Therefore, the judicial review power of the Constitutional Court serves as a tool to check whether organic acts, acts of parliament, emergency decrees, and bills of law are in conflict with the constitutional rights and liberties guaranteed and protected by the provisions of the Constitution.[43] Added to this, Section 213[44]

---

[38] Section 57 (1) of the Constitution of the Kingdom of Thailand (B.E. 2560).

[39] Section 57 (2) of the Constitution of the Kingdom of Thailand (B.E. 2560).

[40] See more on the issue of justiciability of economic social and cultural rights in, e.g., International Commission of Jurists, *Courts and the Legal Enforcement of Economic, Social and Cultural Rights: Comparative Experiences of Justiciability* (2008).

[41] Other state organs established by the Constitution which have a role in protecting fundamental rights include the Courts of Justice and State Attorney Organ.

[42] See more on the structure and power of the Constitutional Court of Thailand and also its controversial role in Thailand's political conflicts in Khemthong Tonsakulrungruang, "The Constitutional Court of Thailand: From Activism to Arbitrariness," *Constitutional Courts in Asia: A Comparative Perspective* (Cambridge University Press 2018).

[43] Please see Sections 148, 173, 212, 231 and 267 of the Constitution of the Kingdom of Thailand (B.E. 2560).

[44] Section 213 of the Constitution of the Kingdom of Thailand provides (B.E. 2560):

of the Constitution sets up a constitutional complaints process via which individuals have direct access to the Constitutional Court in cases where the rights
and liberties guaranteed by the Constitution are violated. However, due to the
conditions set out in the Organic Act on Procedures of the Constitutional Court
B.E. 2561, the channel of direct access is of very limited use.[45] An example of a
possible rare scenario is in a case where an individual, who considers that their
constitutional rights and liberties have been violated as a result of a conflict of
legal provisions with the Constitution, submits a motion to the Ombudsman;
however, the Ombudsman decides not to submit the motion or does not submit
the motion within the stipulated timeframe. In such a case, an individual has
the right to submit the motion directly to the Constitutional Court.[46] Regarding
the Administrative Courts, they possess the competence to try and to adjudicate
the constitutionality of by-laws, including their conformity with the protection
of fundamental rights provided in the constitution and revoke them if they are
found to be unconstitutional.[47]

With respect to the role of the Ombudsmen, they have the power to recommend that relevant State agencies amend any law, by-law, order or any operative
procedure that causes grievance or unfairness or unnecessary or undue burden
on the people.[48] They also have the power to conduct fact-finding in cases of individuals affected by grievance or unfairness arising from non-compliance with

---

"A person whose rights or liberties guaranteed by the Constitution are violated, has the
right to submit a petition to the Constitutional Court for a decision on whether such act is
contrary to or inconsistent with the Constitution, according to the rules, procedures and conditions prescribed by the Organic Act on Procedures of the Constitutional Court."

[45] Section 47 of the Organic Act on Procedures of the Constitutional Court B.E. 2561 (AD
2018).

[46] Section 48 of the Organic Act on Procedures of the Constitutional Court B.E. 2561 (AD
2018).

[47] Section 231 of the Constitution of the Kingdom of Thailand (B.E. 2560) and Sections 11
(2), 43 and 72 of the Act for the Establishment of Administrative Courts and Administrative
Court Procedure, B.E. 2542 (AD 2009)."

[48] Paragraph 1(1) of Section 230 of the Constitution of the Kingdom of Thailand (B.E. 2560).

the law or ultra vires acts of a state agency or state officials in order to make a recommendation for the relevant state agencies to eliminate or deter such grievance or unfairness.[49] However, if it concerns a matter regarding a human right violation, the Ombudsmen shall refer the matter to the National Human Rights Commission for further action.[50] In addition, the Ombudsmen can refer an issue regarding the constitutionality of a provision of law to the Constitutional Court and an issue regarding the legality and constitutionality of a rule, order or any other legal act of a state agency or a state official to the Administrative Court.[51]

Regarding the National Human Rights Commission, it has the duties and powers to examine and report violations of human rights and to suggest suitable measures or guidelines in order to prevent or redress human rights violations to the National Assembly, the Council of Ministers and other relevant state agencies or the private sector. It also has a duty to disseminate the situation of human rights in Thailand to the public and to promote awareness of the importance of human rights in every sector of society.[52] It is worth noting that unlike the Constitution of the Kingdom of Thailand B.E. 2550 (AD 2007), the National Human Rights Commission, according to the current Constitution, is not entitled to submit an issue concerning the constitutionality of provisions of law to the Constitutional Court.

Essentially, this article aims to provide an overview of the structure and legal rules for the guarantee and protection of fundamental rights as well as relevant organs and mechanisms of addressing human rights violations as stipulated in the Constitution of the Kingdom of Thailand B.E 2560 (AD 2017). The Constitution entails a number of specific fundamental rights and liberties as well as key principles such as equal protection, the requirements for the enactment of laws to restrict constitutional rights and liberties, and the immediate effect of the protection of constitutional rights. It also establishes an array of legal mechanisms

---

[49] Paragraph 1(2) of Section 230 of the Constitution of the Kingdom of Thailand (B.E. 2560).

[50] Paragraph 3 of Section 230 of the Constitution of the Kingdom of Thailand (B.E. 2560).

[51] Section 231 of the Constitution of the Kingdom of Thailand (B.E. 2560).

[52] Section 247 of the Constitution of the Kingdom of Thailand (B.E. 2560).

readily available for constitutional organs including the Constitutional Court, the Administrative Courts, the Ombudsman and the National Human Rights Commission to employ to promote and protect fundamental rights. However, the realization of the rights and liberties guaranteed under the Constitution as well as the effectiveness of relevant mechanisms depends on a number of factors, apart from the existence of constitutional provisions and principles as well as relevant constitutional organs and mechanisms. The hope to promote human right standards and alleviate, or even resolve, the problems of human right deterioration in Thailand,[53] especially the serious violations of human rights with respect to the conflict in the southern part of Thailand[54] or Lèse majesté law,[55] lies in the development of democracy, the concept of the rule of law, the concept of the legal state and respect for human/fundamental rights in the political culture and state officials' consciousness as well as the minds of individuals.

---

[53] Please see the human right situations in Thailand in relation to core human right treaties in, e.g., Vitit Muntarbhorn, *Core Human Rights Treaties and Thailand* (Brill Nijhoff).

[54] Please see more on the problem of violations of human rights with respect to the conflict in the southern part of Thailand in, e.g., Andrew Harding and Peter Leyland, *The Constitutional System of Thailand: A Contextual Analysis* (Hart Publishing 2011) 229–232.

[55] Please see more on the problem of violations of human rights regarding or Lèse majesté law in, e.g., ibid 237–247.

Chapter 6

JUDICIAL REVIEW OVER QUASI-JUDICIAL FUNCTIONS AS PROVIDED FOR UNDER THE CONSTITUTIONS OF MYANMAR

Myint Thu Myaing*

(University of Yangon)

1. Characteristics of Myanmar's Constitutional Law

A state is administered by a group of persons known as the government. The government of a state is made up of three branches: the executive, the legislative, and the judiciary. For these three branches to work effectively, some rules and principles must be implemented. Under the authority of these rules and principles, the government is able to administer the state. This set of principles is espoused in what is called the constitution. Therefore, a constitution is the governing wheel of the state. Without it, there would be anarchy in the administration of the state.

The term "constitution" has been variously defined by different authors in line with variable concepts. Aristotle describes a constitution as "the way of life the state has chosen for itself." His definition does not clearly convey the characteristics of a constitution. According to C.F Strong, "A constitution may be said to be a collection of principles according to which the powers of the government, the rights of the government and relation between the two are adjusted." In a wider sense, K.C Wheare explains that the word "constitution is used to denote

---

* Dr. Professor and Head, Department of Law, University of Yangon, Myanmar.

all written and unwritten principles regulating the administration of the state."

According to these authors, a constitution means principles (whether it is written or not) that regulate the administration of a state. Therefore, a constitution is the highest and fundamental law of a state.

Similarly, the constitution is the supreme or higher law in Myanmar. Its provisions provide a framework under which all regulations, legislation, institutions, and procedures operate and express citizen's rights.

Another potentially useful categorization of constitutions is whether they are rigid or flexible. This categorization refers to how easily a constitution can be amended and how easily the constitutional landscape and framework can change. A constitution is said to be rigid when it is difficult to amend or change and flexible when it can be amended more easily.[1]

The Constitution of Myanmar is a constitution with rigid amendment procedures at least in so far as some articles are concerned. Certain provisions are so deeply rooted that amending them requires at least 75% of all members of the Pyithu Hluttaw and a national referendum with the support of over half of all eligible voters in order to be amended.[2] These rigid amendment procedures are placed on provisions related to, among others, basic principles, state structure, and the qualifications of the president and vice president as well as the formation of the Pyidaungsu and the structures of the Pyithu Hluttaw, the Amyotha Hluttaw, and the Region or State Hluttaw.[3]

---

[1] Nora Hedling, International IDEA Constitution Brief, International IDEA's Constitution-Building Primer series, <http://www.constitutionnet.org/primers, October, 2016, p. 2.

[2] Article 436(a), Constitution of Myanmar (2008) "If it is necessary to amend the provisions of Sections 1 to 48 in Chapter I, Sections 49 to 56 in Chapter II, Sections 59 and 60 in Chapter III, Sections 74, 109, 141 and 161 in Chapter IV, Sections 200, 201, 248 and 276 in Chapter V, Sections 293, 294, 305, 314 and 320 in Chapter VI, Sections 410 to 432 in Chapter XI and Sections 436 in Chapter XII of this Constitution, it shall be amended with the prior approval of more than seventy-five percent of all the representatives of the Pyidaungsu Hluttaw, after which in a nation-wide referendum only with the votes of more than half of those who are eligible to vote."

[3] Nora Hedling, International IDEA Constitution Brief, International IDEA's Constitu-

The other characteristic is sometimes drawn from whether a constitution is written or unwritten. This distinction focuses on the nature of a constitution; i.e., whether it is entirely written down and specified in a constitutional document or whether it is a more nebulous body of laws contained in precedents, traditions, customary laws, and practice.[4] Myanmar has adopted a written constitution.

In the Constitution of the Republic of the Union of Myanmar, the three branches' powers are separated to the extent possible and exercise the system of reciprocal control, check, and balance among themselves. In addition, these three branches' powers are also shared among the Union, Regions, States, and Self-Administered Areas.[5]

According to the provisions of the 2008 Constitution, the Union of Myanmar—the official title for the Government of Myanmar—is a unitary presidential constitutional republic. The parliamentary system is bicameral, with a 224-seat Amyotha Hluttaw and a 440-seat Pyithu Hluttaw. The Pyidaungsu Hluttaw comprises of these two Hluttaws. One quarter of all seats in both Hluttaws are assigned to military representatives who serve five-year terms. Sub-nationally, all the seven regions and seven states have elected a unicameral legislature. The executive branch of the government consists of the president, the vice presidents, and minister-level appointees. By law, no executive branch members are members of parliament.[6]

2. Teaching Methods of Constitutional Law in Myanmar

In the fourth year of LLB Course and Civil Law Specialization of LLM Course, students have to be taught constitutional law. Teachers advise students on how to study related statutory laws and law reports to understand the sub-

---

tion-Building Primer series, <http://www.constitutionnet.org/primers, October, 2016, p. 6.

[4] Ibid, p. 2.

[5] Section 11 of the Constitution of the Republic of the Union of Myanmar, 2008.

[6] OECD Open Government Reviews, Myanmar, p-13.

jects thoroughly. They also give students assignments in the form of essays and individual or group presentations. Tutorial teachers direct students and teach them how to write and present their essays and engage them in discussions. In the fourth year of LLB course, constitutional law is taught three times a week for lecture classes and twice a week for tutorial classes. In the LLM course, the lecture time is four times per week and the seminar class takes place twice a week. The duration of each class is 50 minutes. Assessment is based on examination and class work, including attendance, tutorial tests, and paper presentations. There is one paper presentation, six tutorial tests for each subject, and an examination in each semester. The marks distribution for the LLB course is 70/30 (which has been changed from 80/20 to 70/30 starting from 2019–2020 Academic Year); i.e., 70 is for the examination and 30 is for class work., The marks distribution for the LLM course is 70/30. The passing score for the LLB course is 50 out of 100 and for the LLM course, students need to get 65 marks out of 100.

3. Constitutions of Myanmar

Myanmar (erstwhile Burma) regained independence from the British Empire on January 4, 1948. Thereafter, Myanmar has had three constitutions, namely the Constitution of the Union of Burma (1947), the Constitution of the Socialist Republic of the Union of Myanmar (1974), and the Constitution of the Republic of the Union of Myanmar (2008), which is currently in force.

Judicial Review under 1947 Constitution

After independence, the courts established by the Constitution of the Union of Burma (1947) were the Supreme Court and the High Court. The Supreme Court had jurisdiction throughout the whole Union and its decisions were binding on all courts. It was also considered as the court of final appeal for all courts within the Union.

Section 25 of the 1947 Constitution provided citizens with an access to the

Supreme Court to seek protection of their rights by submitting writs. Therefore, the Supreme Court was empowered to check the constitutionality of the activities of the judiciary and executive against the Constitution, as provided by the following Sections:

(1) The right to move the Supreme Court by appropriate proceedings for the enforcement of any of the rights conferred by this Chapter is hereby guaranteed.

(2) Without prejudice to the powers that may be vested in this behalf in other courts, the Supreme Court shall have the power to issue directions in the nature of habeas corpus, mandamus, prohibition, quo warranto, and certiorari appropriate to the rights guaranteed in this Chapter.

(3) The right to enforce these remedies shall not be suspended unless in times of war, invasion, rebellion, insurrection, or grave emergency, as may be required for public safety.

Moreover, Section 4 of the Union Judiciary Act, 1948 gave expansive powers to the Supreme Court to exercise supervise "over all courts in the Union." The Supreme Court was entitled to, on its own motion or if a case was submitted to it, revise and correct any court decision within the Union contrary to the extant legislation.

In terms of the development of the principles of writ applications, the Supreme Court of Burma explicitly cognizant of the fact that the requirements that needed to be satisfied for it to issue the writs had been "borrowed from English law."[7]

In late 1940s and 1950s, the Court placed emphasis on constitutional writs as "means of which this court is empowered to protect and safeguard the person and property of the citizens of the Union."[8]

The writs were therefore depicted as central to accountability and the protection of individual rights against government interference. In terms of comparative jurisprudence, the Supreme Court did consider whether Section 16 of the

---

[7] U Htwe (alias) A E Madari v U Tun Ohn and One [1948] BLR (SC) 541.

[8] Ibid.

1947 Constitution, which guaranteed that no person shall be deprived of his/her personal liberty, could be interpreted with reference to jurisprudence on the due process clause of Section 14(1) of the United States Constitution. The Court ultimately rejected reference to Section 14(1) as irrelevant to the interpretation of the 1947 Constitution.[9]

In the case of *U Pit v Thegon Village Agriculture Committee and two others*,[10] the applicant had been admitted as a tenant of the land in question for some years. The first respondent, Thegon Village Agriculture Committee, had withdrawn this land from the applicant and leased it to the second and third respondents. Under Rule 7 of the Disposal of Tenancies Rules, 1948, a tenant who is in occupation of agricultural land which he cultivated during the agricultural season 1947–1948 shall be permitted to continue to cultivate such land for 1948–1949 also.

Rule 10(2) empowers the Village Agricultural Committee to withdraw such land or a portion thereof from the occupation of such tenant where there are sufficient grounds to believe that he would be unable to cultivate it.

The first respondent made no enquiry and gave him no opportunity to be heard or present his case. The second respondent, Mg Tun Lwin, was a son of U E Maung, who was the secretary of the Thegon Village Agriculture Committee (the first respondent). The court stated that the instructions issued by the government do not prohibit the allotment of land to any relatives of the members of the Committee.

The Village Agricultural Committees are statutory bodies exercising quasi-judicial functions. Therefore, the Committee cannot act in excess of their powers or contrary to the provisions of the Act and rules. These Committees must act according to the rules of natural justice.

The court held that the rule *nisi* in this case is made absolute and the order of

---

[9] Tinzar Maw Naing v The Commissioner of Police Rangoon and others [1950] SC 17, P-23–26.

[10] 1948 BLR (S.C) 759.

the first respondent Committee was quashed. Rule *nisi* means an order obtained ex parte to show cause why it should not be set aside.

In the case of *Ah Kam v U Shwe Phone and others*,[11] the applicant asked for directions in the nature of certiorari and prohibition on the grounds that the amendment of Schedule1 by the insertion of this clause (ချ) was *ultra vires* and that therefore the Special Judge had no jurisdiction to try the case in question. It was held that the president has, by the said amendment, given a carte blanche to the Bureau to pick up and choose in which of those cases it will or will not assume powers and duties and which of those cases it will investigate and send up for trial before the Special Judge. It also empowered the Bureau to decide whether a Special Judge should have powers to try any of the cases. The legislature had confidence in the president and relied upon his administrative wisdom and political sagacity. The president had practically refused to use his judgment and discretion and instead, delegated his powers to the Bureau of Special Investigation. Such delegation was not authorized by the Bureau of Special Investigation Act and it was against the principle that where a trust or discretion in the agent is involved and the exercise of which has been delegated, such agent cannot lawfully appoint another to perform his/her duties. The amendment by insertion of clause (ချ) in the Schedule was found to be *ultra vires* and the Special Judge was not allowed to take cognizance of such cases even after they had been transferred to their courts by the president.

Quasi-judicial Function of Administrative Bodies

A quasi-judicial function, as defined by S.A de Smith, is a "judicial procedure" whereas the decision is made by the discretionary power of the executive.

Therefore, when a body, other than a court, decides a dispute and it is required to follow the elements of judicial procedure and the rules of fair play and natural justice, the process is referred to as quasi-judicial.

The Report of the Committee on Minister's Power (1932) distinguished a

---

[11] 1952 BLR (S.C) 222.

quasi-judicial act from a judicial act, as follows:

A **true judicial decision** presupposes an existing dispute between two or more parties and then involves four requisites:-

(1) The presentation (not necessarily orally) of the case by the parties to the dispute;

(2) If the dispute between them is a question of fact, the ascertainment of the fact by means of evidence adduced by the parties to the dispute and often with the assistance of arguments by or on behalf of the parties on the evidence;

(3) If the dispute between them is a question of law, the submission of legal arguments by the parties; and

(4) A decision which disposes of the whole matter by a finding upon the facts in dispute and an application of the law of the land to the facts so found, including where a ruling upon any disputed question of law is required.

A **quasi-judicial decision** equally presupposes an existing dispute between two or more parties and involves points (1) and (2), but it does not necessarily involve point (3) and never involves (4).

In the opinion of the Committee, the essential distinction between a judicial and a quasi- judicial function is that in the former, there is no element of discretion whereas there is invariably statutory permission to exercise discretion in the performance of a quasi-judicial function.

A definition of quasi-judicial was given by **Lord Atkin J** in the famous case of *The King v Electricity Commissioners Ex parte London Electricity Join Committee Co.*[12] Lord Atkin's test for judicial control consists of three parts, which are:

(1) having legal authority

(2) to determine questions affecting the rights of subjects

(3) having the duty to act judicially.

In Myanmar, this test was considered in the case of *U Htwe (a) A.E Madari v U Tun Ohn*[13]. In this case, it was established that the meaning of a court can be

---

[12] 1924, 1 KB 171.
[13] 1948 BLR (SC) 541.

controlled by the superior court where the court:

1. has legal authority
2. determines questions affecting the rights of subjects
3. has the duty to act according to law and
4. acts in excess of his or their legal authority, those writs will be issued.

Therefore, the view of Lord Atkin was varied only on the third point. In Myanmar, the third point is "having the duty to act according to law" while in Lord Atkin's view is "having the duty to act judicially."

The Doctrine of Judicial Review

The doctrine of judicial review of administrative actions is incorporated in the various constitutional provisions. Judicial review and control of administrative actions provide a fundamental safeguard against abuse of power and discretion.

Where appeals from decisions of administrative bodies are brought in courts, the courts can declare such decisions invalid or quash them if they are *ultra vires*. For example, if an appeal against the decision of the income tax commission is brought to court seeking to have an order of exaggerating taxes quashed. In this case, the court will have to consider for two main points: "grounds for review" and "methods of review."[14]

The Grounds for Review

A judicial review is completely different from a system of appeals because it is not based on the merits but on the legality of the lower authority's proceedings. If the root of the matter is jurisdiction or *intra vires* and no appeal from it is provided by statute, then it is immune from control by a court of law. However, if a body exceeds or abuses its powers, so that it is acting *ultra vires*, then a court of law can quash its decision by declaring it to be legally invalid.[15]

---

[14] Department of Law, University of Distance Education, Administrative Law, Part I, Series No. (635), 1995, p. 65.

[15] H.W.R Wade, Administrative Law, 1961, The Clarendon Press, Oxford, P-43.

The grounds for review can be considered from three main perspectives, which include:

(1) jurisdictional matters

(2) error of law on the face of record

(3) the rules of natural justice

(1) Jurisdictional Matters

Jurisdiction means the authority to decide matters, and this is examined from the perspective of a body having the authority or jurisdiction to decide a matter. Acting *ultra vires* and acting without jurisdiction have essentially the same meaning.

There are three kinds of jurisdictional matters:

(a) excess of jurisdiction

(b) lack of jurisdiction

(c) refusal to exercise jurisdiction

(2) Error of Law on the Face of Record

Where, upon the face of record, it appears that the determination of the inferior tribunal is wrong in law, an order of certiorari will be granted.

A simple example of review on the grounds of error of law on the face is *R, V Minister of Housing and Local Government, Ex. P Chichester R. D. C.*[16] The Minister was found to have applied the wrong test in coming to his decision. The decisions were then quashed by an order of certiorari on the basis of that error of law.

(3) The Rules of Natural Justice

The rules of natural justice are categorized in two:

(1) The rule against bias and

(2) The right to a hearing[17]

---

[16] (1969) 2 ALL E.R. 407.

[17] Department of Law, University of Distance Education, Administrative Law, Part I, Series

Methods of Review

A review may take place incidentally in the course of prosecution for an offense under a statutory regulation, thereby showing that the regulation is *ultra vires*. Apart from review in the course of ordinary litigation, there are several means of directly invoking the jurisdiction of the courts to check excess or abuse of powers.

The principal machinery of reviewing quasi-judicial functions is provided by prerogative writs; certiorari, prohibition, and mandamus writs. These prerogative writs are the derived from the special powers of the Crown and they are primarily concerned with the Crown. The writ of habeas corpus has always been issued upon the application of subjects since time in memorial. The Supreme Court has powers to issue directions in the nature of habeas corpus, mandamus, prohibition, quo warranto, and certiorari.

Certiorari

The writ of certiorari is a writ issued in writing as a decision that is in conformity with the law if it is found that the decision of any court or any quasi-judicial matter is not in conformity with the law.[18]

It is issued whenever a tribunal acts without jurisdiction or patently in excess of jurisdiction, when there is an error on the face of the record, or when its proceedings are conducted in a manner contrary to the rules of natural justice.

The object of a writ of certiorari is to bring up the records of an inferior court, an administrative tribunal, or other administrative bodies discharging some quasi-judicial functions for examination before a superior court so that it may be certified if their (inferior courts, administrative tribunals, or other administrative bodies) work and acts are within their jurisdiction and they do not exceed the limits of jurisdiction specified by the law. The writ is then issued to correct, quash, or remove the acts and the effects of the acts of the inferior court

---

No. (635), 1995, p. 69.

[18] Section 2(g) of the Law Relating to the Application of Writ, 2014.

or tribunal when the acts are judicial or quasi-judicial.

However, the writ is not issued against anybody if the functions performed by are ministerial and administrative.

In Myanmar, the adopted definition of the writ of certiorari is that of C.J Ba U., in *U Htwe (alia) A.E Madari V U Tun Ohn and another*[19], that "the writ of certiorari is a writ issued by superior Court in the exercise of its superintending power over inferior jurisdiction and its superintending power over inferior jurisdiction and it requires judges or officers of such jurisdiction to certify or send proceeding before them to the superior Court for the purpose of examination as to their legality or giving more satisfactory effect to them."

Prohibition

The writ of prohibition means a writ issued in writing not to perform beyond the jurisdiction (*ultra vires*) or against justice in any proceeding of any court or any quasi-judicial matter.[20]

A writ of prohibition is a judicial writ or process issued by a superior court directed to an inferior court for the purposes of preventing the inferior court from usurping a jurisdiction.

Prohibition is usually applied to the court together with the certiotari. Certiorari quashes a decision which has been made while prohibition seeks to prevent or prohibit a body from acting.

Mandamus

The writ of mandamus is a writ issued in writing requiring any competent person, authority, government department, etc. to comply with the law or fulfill their statutory or public obligations.[21] The prerogative remedy of mandamus is the most generally used weapon for compelling performance of public duties.

---

[19] 1948 BLR 541 S.C.

[20] Section 2(e) of the Law Relating to the Application of Writ, 2014.

[21] Section 2(d) of the Law Relating to the Application of Writ, 2014.

The purpose of the writ is to enforce any specific legal right, which is infringed by non-performance from an officer or any other authority in instances where no specific legal remedy is provided by law.

Mandamus is issued when a petitioner satisfies that following requirements:

(i) that he/she has a legal right

(ii) that they have already demanded the performance but the authority refused to act and

(iii)   that there is no effective alternative remedy

A legal right of the petitioner alone creates a legal duty, which a public authority may be required to perform. Therefore, existence of a legal right must be shown.

Habeas Corpus

The writ of habeas corpus is a writ issued in writing requiring a detainee to be brought to court in order to determine whether or not the detention is in conformity with law. It is issued by any court of the Republic of the Union of Myanmar or any competent authority.[22]

Therefore, this writ protects personal liberty or physical integrity by means of a judicial decree ordering the appropriate authorities to bring the detained person before a judge so that the lawfulness of the detention may be determined and, if appropriate, the release of the detainee ordered.[23]

Quo Warranto

The writ of quo warranto is a writ issued in writing requiring any person, any government department, or any authority to which it is directed to show that it has carried out its functions in accordance with the existing laws, rules, regulations, by-laws, procedures, orders, notifications, and directives.[24] It is issued

---

[22] Section 2(c), Ibid.

[23] International Commission of Jurists, Handbook on Habeas Corpus in Myanmar, Geneva, Switzerland, 2016, p-1.

[24] Section 2(f) of the Law Relating to the Application of Writ, 2014.

based on the information filed in a court with a view to try the title to an office, liberty, or privilege.

The office to which the claim is examined must be a public office. It examines the claim which a person asserts to an office, and if the claim is not well founded it can oust the office holder from their official position.

It is not issued as a matter of right; it is a discretionary relief which can only be sought by a person who has suffered a personal injury.[25]

Judicial Review under the 1974 Constitution

Until 1962, over 250 writ cases had been heard. The writ of certiorari was the most common remedy sought by applicants during this period. Many cases also concerned the writ of habeas corpus.

On 2nd March 1962, the Revolutionary Council took over the state power and the judicial system was transformed into a socialist system. The legislative, executive, and judicial powers were vested in the hands of the Chairman of the Revolutionary Council. On April 1, 1962, the two former Courts of Appeal—the High Court and the Supreme Court—were abolished and their powers and functions were amalgamated into one newly established court, known as the Chief Court, which continued to function as the highest court of appeal in both civil and criminal matters in Yangon city. Notification No. 25 of the Revolutionary Council granted the Chief Court powers to issue only the writ of certiorari. Subordinate courts remained unchanged until 1972. On August 17, 1972, the People's Judiciary system was introduced. Courts were composed of representatives of the council of workers and peasants. In addition, various judicial committees were established and granted jurisdiction over criminal and civil matters.

The 1974 Constitution of the Socialist Republic of the Union of Myanmar came into force on January 3, 1974. The Council of People's Justice was the highest organ of the judiciary. Further, the 1974 socialist Constitution no longer

---

[25] Mangal Chandra Jain Kagzi, "The India Administrative Law", First Edition, 1962, Metropolitan Book Co. (Private) Ltd. Delhi. P-155.

provided for writs, and the power to conduct constitutional review of legislations was taken away from the courts.

In 1988, when the State Law and Order Restoration Council took power, the new regime continued a pattern of interfering with the structure of the courts and the appointment and term of the judiciary. It established a new court system with a Supreme Court, although it did not grant the Supreme Court the powers to hear and determine writ cases.

The State Peace and Development Council was instituted in 1997. The Judiciary Law 2000 was then promulgated by the council. According to the provisions of this Law, the Supreme Court was still the highest judicial organ of the Union of Myanmar. However, the writ jurisdiction could not be exercised by the Supreme Court during that reign of the State Peace and Development Council.

Judicial Review under 2008 Constitution

In Myanmar, under the military rule (1962–2008), there was no effective mechanism of challenging the lawfulness of detention before a court. A major (and unanticipated) improvement in Myanmar's 2008 Constitution was the reintroduction of the writs. Since then, the government has passed the "Law relating to Application of Writs 2014" and the Supreme Court has promulgated rules and procedures for its implementation.[26]

The right to issue writs under the 2008 Constitution is conferred upon the Supreme Court of the Union. The Constitution, therefore, allows for access to the writs to challenge the legality of decisions of lower courts and of government agencies. Currently, there is no opportunity for individuals to bring writ cases to the State and Region High Courts; this right is only available in the Supreme Court. The jurisdiction of the Supreme Court to issue writs is contained in Section 296, which stipulates that the Supreme Court of the Union:

(a) has the power to issue the following writs:

---

[26] International Commission of Jurists, Handbook on Habeas Corpus in Myanmar, Geneva, Switzerland, 2016, p-1.

(i)   Habeas Corpus

(ii)   Mandamus

(iii) Prohibition

(iv) Quo Warranto

(v)   Certiorari

(b) The application to issue writs shall be suspended in areas where a state of emergency is declared.

This provision has a similar effect to Section 25 of the 1947 Constitution. Legal practitioners in Myanmar view this provision as essentially reviving the right to the writs that was formerly provided under the 1947 Constitution. While many aspects of the 2008 Constitution have been criticized, Section 296 on the writs is regarded by many as an important and democratic aspect of the Constitution.

The jurisdiction of the Supreme Court of the Union to issue writs, including the writ of habeas corpus, is reiterated in Chapter VIII of the 2008 Constitution, which provides for Fundamental Rights and Duties of Citizens. Section 378 expressly states that "in connection with the filing for the application of rights granted" by the Constitution, the Supreme Court has the power to issue writs. Notwithstanding the shortcomings of the 2008 Constitution, the recognition of writs under Chapter VIII is a positive step toward achieving the rule of law in the country. Section 378 confirms that habeas corpus is a fundamental right protected by the constitution. While Sections 353 and 367 of the 2008 Constitution protect against arbitrary detention and provide a right to be brought before a court, habeas corpus allows individuals to challenge the legality of their detention. The inclusion of habeas corpus brings the Constitution closer to international standards that reiterate the right of all persons deprived of their liberty "to take proceedings before a court, in order that that court may decide without delay on the lawfulness of his detention and order his release if the detention is not lawful." Before the writ law and procedure were developed, the Supreme Court had jurisdiction to issue writs under the Union Judiciary Law. The procedural rules for the application of writs were developed between 2011 and 2013. In June 2014, the Law on the Application for Writs 24/2014 (writ law) was enacted to codify the procedure—it sets out limited definitions, duties, and responsibilities concerning all procedural writs. Although it is narrow in its focus, the writ law is significant as it provides an indication of current understandings of the doctrine of separation of powers and the role of the courts.[27]

Some Cases Related to Writs under the 2008 Constitution

In *Daw Than Than Htay and two others v Judge of High Court of Region, High Court of Magway Region, and seven others,*[28] the court stated that when applying for the issue of a writ, the application should be supported by an affidavit fully stating the reasons why it is being applied for and certifying that all facts therein are true.

The Supreme Court of the Union examines the application and affidavit (not like an original court which calls directly examines a witness) to determine whether the order passed by an inferior court is contrary to law or not and whether it is appropriate to issue a writ or not. This was also reiterated in the case of *Chan U Ta (applicant) v Permanent Secretary, Ministry of Foreign Affairs, Yangon and another.* In this case, upon examining the application and attached affidavit submitted by the applicants, the High Court of the Region dismissed the application. The applicants then submitted an appeal to the High Court of Magawy Region, but the appeal was also dismissed because the High Court of Magawy Region found that the orders of the High Court of the Region were valid and within the Region Court's jurisdiction. Therefore, there was no reason to issue a writ against orders that were not contrary to the law.

The writ of certiorari was issued in the case of *Daw Myint Yee and another v Administrator of Township (General Administration Department, Shwe Kyin Township) (2013)*[29]. In this case, the Township's administrator detained the applicants in a civil prison and the Head of Township Police Force and the jailer of

---

[27] International Commission of Jurists, Handbook on Habeas Corpus in Myanmar, Geneva, Switzerland, 2016, p-16.

[28] 2011 MLR 127.

[29] 2013 Civil Miscellaneous case No. 121.

Prison Department (Bago) kept them without any prison warrant. The applicants then applied for a writ of certiorari and a writ of habeas corpus since the respondents' actions were illegal. According to the statement of head of Township Land Record Department, the disputed land that the applicants squatted was obviously recognized as the land at the disposal of the government under the Lower Burma (Myanmar) Town and Village Land Act, 1898.

Therefore, there were no facts showing that the disputed land belonged to the state. However, the appellee No. 1 took action against the applicants under Section 21 of the Lower Burma (Myanmar) Town and Village Land Act, 1898 and issued an arrest warrant under Section 21 (2) of the same Act and passed an order to detain them in Bago Prison for 30 days. However, this order was not legal.

As per the law of Myanmar, a writ shall be issued when the orders of any subordinate court or administrative authorities undertaking quasi-judicial functions are wrong and affect the legal rights of citizens. Therefore, this application was allowed with costs to the applicants. The order to detain the applicants in civil prison for 30 days under Section 21 (2) of the Lower Burma (Myanmar) Town and Village Land Act, 1898 passed by the Deputy Collector and the warrant to detain them on 25.3.2013 were also set aside.

Consequently, it is clear that writs, including the writ of certiorari, can be exercised over administrative bodies exercising judicial power.

Professor Dr. Daw Kyin Htay v Union Minister for the Ministry of Education of 2013[30] was the first case in which a writ of certiorari was issued and in which the Supreme Court quashed the administrative decision made by the Ministry of Education. The applicant was Daw Kyin Htay, who was then a professor and the Head of the Economic of Education Department of Yangon University of Distance Education. She was forced to retire by a ministerial order without any right to be heard, to explain, or to appeal. It was argued that the decision of the Minister of Education was *ultra vires* the power of the Minister endowed by the Civil Service Personnel Law. This case was followed by many similar cases that

---

[30] 2013 Civil Miscellaneous case No. 290.

sought remedy to administrative actions that were *ultra vires*.

In the case of *U Kyaw Myint v Daw Tin Hla*,[31] a judgment and decree of Pabe-than Township Court and Yangon Western District Court, where the applicant applied for a writ of certiorari and a writ of prohibition, it was held that these two writs were one before the Union Judiciary Law, 2010. Therefore, the court had no right to issue writ of certiorari and prohibition by means of retrospection against such judgment and decree, which in this case was U Kyaw Hla, under Sections 16 (A) (3) and (5) of the Union Judiciary Law.

The applicant stated in his application that he had applied on 27.12.2010 to submit civil revision on the judgment and decree of the Pabetan Township Court and the Yangon Western District Court in accordance with Section 115 proviso (2) of Civil Procedure Code. The Supreme Court of the Union dismissed the application because the writs of certiorari and prohibition have to be applied for within three months. If it is not sought within this time limit, then the writs of certiorari and prohibition will not be issued as per paragraph 61 of the Writ Pro-cedure Rules and Regulations. This implies that the court will only consider the application if the writ of certiorari or the writ of prohibition is applied for within three months.

In *U Myint Than and five others v The Republic of the Union of Myanmar and two others*,[32] it was stated that the case was an application for the writ of pro-hibition. The High Court of Mandalay Region, as the Revision Court according to Section 522 (3) of Criminal Procedure Code, had power to issue orders just like the original court under Section 522 (3) of Criminal Procedure Code.

When issuing a writ, the Supreme Court of the Union has to be cautious not to interfere in a case in which the subordinate court has power to decide within its own jurisdiction.

If the applicants are not satisfied with the order of the High Court of Manda-lay Region, they can apply for revision to the Supreme Court of the Union.

---

[31] 2011 MLR 1.
[32] 2011 MLR 127.

After the Supreme Court hears the writ application case, if there is no reason to make preliminary decisions for the defendants to show cause, then it rejects the application to issue the writ of prohibition.

A writ of mandamus was issued in the case of *Daw Tin Nwet v Collector (District Administrator) General Administration Department of Tangoo and three others*[33]. In this case, the collector passed an order to revoke a grant that was in the applicant's name and categorized her land as state land without examining her. Therefore, she applied for a writ of mandamus against this collector's order.

In this case, with regard to the change and issuance of grant land, which was in the name of the applicant's father, it had not been shown that any interested persons lodged any appeal within the limited timeframe under Rule 136 of the Lower Burma Land and Revenue Rules and Rule 75 (1) of the Lower Burma Towns and Village Lands Rules.

Nevertheless, the Director General of the General Administration Department, who was using the revision powers under Section 40 of the Lower Burma Towns and Village Lands Act, instructed the District General Administrator to revoke the applicant's grant. The former did not give any reasons for revoking this grant and there were no facts indicating that the applicant broke the rules or that she fraudulently applied for the grant. Therefore, at that time, she was allowed to get the grant. Fifteen years later, the respondents gave out instructions for the grant to be revoked without according her the opportunity to be heard. This infringes upon the rights of defense as provided for by the Constitution under citizens' rights. Therefore, revoking the grant, which was in the name of the applicant, did not appear to be consistent with the authority given by law. As a result, the Supreme Court set aside the instructions by issuing the writ of mandamus.

Therefore, this civil application was allowed with costs to the applicant and the instructions issued by the District ~~General~~ Administration Department on

---

[33] 2015 Civil Miscellaneous Case No. 41.

23.1.2015 were set aside and the order for acquiring the applicant's land as the state land dismissed.

The writs of mandamus and quo warranto were also issued in the case of *U Than Aung and three others v Markets Department (Yangon City Development Committee) and another*[34]. When the Thingunkyun Market was destroyed by fire, a two-story R.C Building was built by the Markets Department in coopera-tion with Aung Kaung Kyaw Company. That building made transportation dif-ficult and it did not take into consideration fire safety measures. As a result, the applicants sought the writs of mandamus and quo warranto against the respond-ents.

There were no disputed facts as pertains to the disputed land which was presented by the application and mentioned as public land in the Block Map. In addition, the disputed land was not included in the Yangon City Development Committee Lands or Lands at the Disposal of the Committee or plots of land and reserved land. There was also no provision stipulating that the Committee can change and stipulate that public land is its own land under Section 11 (y) of the Yangon City Development Committee Law (Functions and Duties of Commit-tee). Therefore, in order to record the land history, the decision that lands beside market areas (0.257 acres) were considered as lands of the market area was not in line with Section 11(y), the Chapter 3 of the Yangon City Development Commit-tee Law, 2013, and Rule 16 of the City Planning and Land Administration Rule under the Notification No (3/2001).

Therefore, the construction of the two-story R.C Building, which had been built on the disposal land (12'×80') by Thingunkyun Market Office and East Dis-trict Markets Department of Y.C.D.C, was not consistent with Rules 39 and 43 of the Y.C.D.C Roads and Bridges Rule. As a result, the court found it necessary to issue a writ of quo warranto.

From the above cases, it can be concluded that writs are the only means of seeking judicial review of administrative decisions in Myanmar, and only the

---

[34] 2014 Civil Miscellaneous case No. 118.

highest court of Myanmar can issue writs and has the jurisdiction to try writ applications.

Chapter 7

CONSTITUTION AND CONSTITUTIONAL REVIEW IN MYANMAR

Khin Phone Myint Kyu*
(University of Yangon)

1. Constitutions in Myanmar

Myanmar was annexed by the British on January 1, 1886. Since then, the British legal system, laws, and rules have influenced Myanmar's legal system. It is based on the common law legal system. On April 1, 1937, Myanmar was separated from India and a new constitution was accorded to her by the Government of Burma (Myanmar) Act 1935. In 1942, Burma (Myanmar) was attacked by Japanese forces. During the Japanese occupation, Myanmar was administered under martial law. The British Government issued a statement of policy in May 1945, which envisaged a return to the 1935 Constitution after three years of military government. In August 1945, Myanmar was re-administered by the British Empire. In every response to the British Government's policy, Myanmar demanded for complete independence. The elections for a Constituent Assembly were held in April 1947, and the Anti-Fascist People's Freedom League (AFPFL) won. The Constituent Assembly met in June 1947 to draft the Constitution of Myanmar. The Constitution was adopted by the Assembly in September 1947 and Myanmar

---

* Professor, Department of Law, University of Yangon, Myanmar.

gained her independence on January 4, 1948. The Constitution of the Union of Burma 1947 was operating on the Independence Day of Myanmar. This was the first constitution in Myanmar after independence.

During this time, the courts established by the 1947 Constitution were the Supreme Court and the High Court. According to the 1947 Constitution, Myanmar was included in the category of the parliamentary executive of the Union Government.

On March 2, 1962, the Revolutionary Council took over the state power, including legislative, executive, and judicial powers, which was vested in the hands of the chairperson of the Revolutionary Council. In July 1971, a decision was made by the first Convention of the Myanmar Socialist Programme Party to draw a new Constitution. In October 1973, a new draft Constitution was adopted by the Party Convention, and a referendum was held in December 1973. Majority of the people supported and accepted the Constitution. The new Constitution came into force on January 3, 1974 as the Constitution of the Socialist Republic of the Union of Myanmar.

In 1988, there was general discontent among the people had risen due to economic declination, leading to a countrywide civil disturbance and the administrative machinery broke down. On September 18, 1988 the State Law and Order Restoration Council (SLORC) took over the state power and it suspended the 1974 Constitution and abolished various councils, key among them being the Pyithu Hluttaw.

The SLORC called for a National Convention in 1993 but it was suspended in 1996. The National Convention was called again in 2004 to draft a new Constitution. The National Convention Convening Commission was formed under Order 12/1992 of the SLORC on October 2, 1992. To convene the National Convention and lay down the fundamental principles of drafting an enduring Constitution of the State, the Commission formed two committees: the National Convention Convening Work Committee and National Convention Convening Management Committee.

The Work Committee was tasked with laying down detailed principles for drafting a new constitution. It comprised of 27 members and the Work Committee formed eight groups, namely: Representatives of Registered Political Parties Group, Representatives of elected political persons group, Representatives of the Nationalities Group, Representatives of the Peasantry Group, Representatives of the Workers Group, Representatives of the Intellectual and Intelligentsia Group, Representatives of the State Service Personnel Group, and Other Suitable Invited Persons Group. Members of these groups were well experienced in various aspects of politics, security, administration, economics, social issues, and the law. The process of laying down the principles was successfully completed on September 3, 2007, after approving 104 basic principles in the National Convention. The State Peace and Development Council issued Announcement No. 2/2007, which formed the Commission for Drafting the State Constitution on October 18, 2007 and gave it the mandate to draft a new Constitution. The final draft was concluded in 2008, and the State Peace and Development Council issued a notification to hold a referendum on the draft Constitution.

Consequently, a national referendum was held on May 10, 2008. After that referendum, the State Peace and Development Council announced that the Constitution of the Republic of the Union of Myanmar has been ratified and promulgated by the referendum under Announcement No. 7/2008 on May 29, 2008. Myanmar had been a sovereign state without a constitution from 1988 to 2008.

The 2008 Constitution consists of 15 chapters, including a Preamble, 457 sections, and five schedules.

2. Characteristics of the 2008 Constitution

The Republic of the Union of Myanmar is constituted by the Union System[1] and the Union has embraced a genuine, disciplined multi-party democratic system.[2] The three branches of the sovereign power are separated, to the extent

---

[1] Section 8, the Constitution of the Republic of the Union of Myanmar, 2008.

[2] Section 7, Ibid.

possible, and exert reciprocal control, check, and balance among themselves. In addition, those separated sovereign powers are shared among the Union, regions, states, and self-administered areas.[3]

In the legislative branch, Pyidaungsu Hluttaw is the highest organ and it consists of two Hluttaws: the Pyithu Hluttaw and the Amyotha Hluttaw. In both Hluttaws, 25% of the representatives are military personnel who are nominated by the Commander-In-Chief of the Defence Services in accordance with the law. In addition, the legislative powers are also shared to the Region Hluttaws and State Hluttaws. Legislative power which is stipulated by the Constitution shall be shared to the Self-Administered Areas.[4]

Section 16 of the Constitution has provided the guiding principle for the establishment of the system of government. According to this section, the President is the Head of the State and the Head of the Union Government. The President takes precedence over all other persons throughout the Republic of the Union of Myanmar.[5]

The Presidential Electoral College is tasked with the responsibility of electing the President. The college is formed with three groups of the Pyidaungsu Hluttaw representatives.[6] Therefore, the President is elected by the Pyidaungsu Hluttaw representatives; in other words, the President elected by the legislature, not by nation-wide presidential elections. Therefore, the system of Government is said to be in the rule of a parliamentary system or parliamentary executive.

The Union Government is comprised of the President, Vice President, Ministers of the Union, and the Attorney-General of the Union.[7] The Union Government does not have a Prime Minister. Therefore, the system of Government is a "Presidential Executive" system.

Courts of the Union consist of ordinary courts of various levels, the

---

[3] Section 11, Ibid.
[4] Section 12(a), Ibid.
[5] Section 58, Ibid.
[6] Section 60, Ibid.
[7] Section 200, Ibid.

Courts-Martial and the Constitutional Tribunal of the Union.[8] Among the ordinary courts, the Supreme Court of the Union is the highest court in the Union. In exercising its jurisdiction, the Supreme Court is required to be cautious not to affect the power of the Constitutional Tribunal of the Union and the Courts-Martial.

With regard to the amendment of the Constitution, it is provided in Chapter XII of the Constitution. Any provision of the Constitution may be amended by submitting a proposal in the form of a Bill.[9] The Bill to amend the Constitution shall be submitted to the Pyidaungsu Hluttaw.[10] If 20% of the total numbers of Pyidaungsu Hluttaw representatives submit the Bill, it shall be considered by the Pyidaungsu Hluttaw.[11] Relating to the basic principles of the Union, state structure, qualification of the President and the Vice President, election of the President, formation of the Pyidaungsu Hluttaw, the Pyithu Hluttaw, the Amyotha Hluttaw, the Region or the State Hluttaw, Union Government, National Defence and Security Council, Region or State Government, Leading Bodies of Self-Administered Division and Zone, formation of courts, composition of the Supreme Court of the Union, formation of the High Court of the Region or State, Constitution of the Constitutional Tribunal of the Union, provisions on state of emergency and amendment provisions, it shall be amended with the prior approval of more than 75% of all the representatives of the Pyidaungsu Hluttaw, after which a nation-wide referendum will follow and the amendments shall pass with the votes of more than half of those who are eligible to vote.[12]

Other provisions shall be amended only by a vote of more than 75% of all the representatives of the Pyidaungsu Hluttaw.

Therefore, a Bill for amendment is initiated in the Pyidaungsu Hluttaw through submission of a Bill, with the support of at least 20% of its members.

---

[8] Section 293, Ibid.
[9] Section 433, the Constitution of the Union of Myanmar.
[10] Section 434, Ibid.
[11] Section 435, Ibid.
[12] Section 436(a), Ibid.

These provisions are divided into two categories for the purposes of amendment, and both require more than 75% of all its members for adoption and some provisions will also require the support of a referendum of more than 50% of all those who are eligible to vote. Consequently, it can be said that the 2008 Constitution is a rigid Constitution.

3. Teaching Constitutional Law in Myanmar

In Myanmar, basic education is divided into primary education, middle school education, and high school education. This amounts to 12 years of education terms after the completion of kindergarten.[13] Therefore, Myanmar has adopted a5-4-3 education system. Compulsory free education has been implemented at the primary level and it shall be extended gradually to higher grades. In the next academic year (2020–2021), basic constitutional concepts will be taught from grade six to grade twelve in the Civic and Moral Subject.

In higher levels of learning, constitutional law is taught in the specializations of law and international relations under graduate and Master of Laws programs.

In the Bachelor of Laws (LLB) programs, constitutional law is taught during the first semester of fourth year as a compulsory subject. This unit mainly covers the State and the Constitution, classification of the Constitution, the 1947 Constitution, the 1974 Constitution, and the 2008 Constitution. It is taught thrice a week for lecture classes and twice a week for tutorial classes. The credit units for this subject are four and the marks distribution is 70/30, which means that 70 for exams and 30 for tests. In the master program, this unit is taught in civil law specialization, and it is studied for two semesters. The program covers the theory and practices of constitutional law of worldwide nations. It is taught four times per week for lecture classes and twice a week for tutorial classes. The credit units for this subject are four and the marks distribution is 70/30. In both under-

---

[13] Section 16(a), National Education Law, 2014.

graduate and master programs, assessment is based on examination and class work through attendance, tutorial tests, and paper presentation. The duration of the classes is normally 50 minutes per class.

4. Constitutional Review in Myanmar

Constitutional review is the process of determining questions related to constitutional interpretation, the constitutionality of laws, executive acts and acts of political parties, and elections based on statutory procedures and in specific ways as provided by the Constitution. Constitutions across the world have devised two broad types of constitutional review; i.e., constitutional review is either carried out either by a specialized court or by a court of general legal jurisdiction.[14] Constitutional review carried out by a court of general legal jurisdiction is called a "judicial review."

Under Section 11 of the Constitution, the Union of Myanmar exercises separation of powers and a multilevel governance system. Therefore, it can be considered that the Union of Myanmar has adopted the constitutional review technique propagated by the multilevel governance theory.

4.1 The Institution Authorized to Exercise the Power of Constitutional Review

The concept of establishing a separate court to settle questions related to the Constitution did not take into account the provisions of the previous two constitutions. However, according to Section 151 of the 1947 Constitution, the Supreme Court had power to decide constitutional disputes and interpret the Constitution. Moreover, under Section 153 of that Constitution, the Supreme Court was granted additional powers to implement the Constitution, as it was deemed necessary

---

[14] International IDEA, Constitution Brief, October, 2016. P. 1, www.idea.int'@2016 International IDEA

by Parliament.

After the adoption of the 1974 Constitution, the Pyithu Hluttaw became the institution mandated to review and decide constitutional issues—under Article 200 and Article 201 of the 1974 Socialist Constitution.

The 2008 Constitution sets separation of powers among the three institutions; the executive, the legislature and the judiciary. If these three institutions happen to have disputes with each other, the prescribed duties and powers of each branch are used as the determining factors to resolve the disputes. In Myanmar, such disputes are heard and determined by the Constitutional Tribunal of the Union. Therefore, Myanmar uses a centralized model of dispute resolution because it is a separate institution to settle the constitutional disputes.

The Tribunal was established in 2011 along with a series of democratic transitions after the country had been under the military government for nearly three decades due to constitutional disputes. The Tribunal is the very first of its kind in Myanmar and started to operate on March 30, 2011.

The Tribunal is considered as a special court.[15] Therefore, it stands as separate judicial institution in Myanmar. Moreover, it was established to exercise exclusive jurisdiction over constitutional matters.[16]

4.2 The Appointment and Removal Process of Judges

The Tribunal is constituted of nine members, key among them being the chairperson.[17] The President of the Union has the mandate to appoint the chairperson and members of the Tribunal, who are subsequently approved by the Pyidaungsu Hluttaw.[18] In particular, the President, the Speaker of Pyithu Hluttaw, and the Speaker of Amyotha Hluttaw each choose three members,[19] who are qualified as described in Section 333 of the Constitution and serve for a term of

---

[15] Section 293(c) , the Constitution of the Republic of the Union of Myanmar.

[16] Section 46, Ibid.

[17] Section 320, Ibid.

[18] Section 327, Ibid.

[19] Section 321, Ibid.

five years.[20]

The qualifications of the members of the Tribunal are:

(a) Person who has attained the age of 50 years;

(b) Person who has qualifications, with the exception of the age limit, prescribed in Section 120 for Pyithu Hluttaw representatives;

(c) Person whose qualification does not breach the provisions under Section 121 which disqualify a person standing for decision as Pyithu Hluttaw representatives;

(d) (i) person who has served as a Judge of the High Court of the Region or the State for at least five years; or

(ii) person who has served as a Judicial Officer or a Law Officer at least 10 years not lower than that of the Region or State level for; or

(iii) person who has practiced as an Advocate for at least 20 years; or

(iv) person who is in the opinion of the President, an eminent jurist.

(e) Person who is not a member of a political party;

(f) Person who is not a Hluttaw representative;

(g) Person who has a political, administrative, economic, and security outlook;

(h) Person loyal to the Union and its citizens.[21]

In 2016, U Sai Than Maung Naing, a member of Amyotha Hluttaw and 22 other members submitted to the Tribunal a matter relating to the qualification of its members.[22] In their submissions, one of their main issues was the qualifications of the Tribunal's members, which says that "person who is, in the opinion of the President, an eminent jurist." They also requested for an interpretation on whether this provision is applicable only to the three members chosen by the President under Section 321 of the Constitution.

In this submission, there were three main issues:

---

[20] Section 335, Ibid.

[21] Section 333, the Constitution of the Republic of the Union of Myanmar.

[22] Submission No. 1/2016.

(a) Whether the treatment of the Pyidaungsu Hluttaw as a respondent in the case is contrary to the law or not;

(b) Whether the interpretation of the action which is decided and approved by the Pyidaungsu Hluttaw is contrary to the law or not and whether the Constitutional Tribunal has jurisdiction over Pyidaungsu Hluttaw's resolutions;

(c) Whether the new additional formation and expansion of the Tribunal's law with respect to Section 333(d)(iv) is contrary to the Constitution.

The Tribunal decided that it has the power to scrutinize the constitutionality of the laws enacted by the legislature and the actions or measures of executive authorities. However, the authority to conduct a constitutional review over the actions or measures of the legislature is not vested. The Tribunal further decided that the actions and decisions of the Pyidaungsu Hluttaw are not within its competence. The Tribunal also held that the changing and expanding of the original formation of Section 4(b) of the Constitutional Tribunal of the Union Law was contrary to the Constitution and dismissed the submission.

The chairperson and the members of the Tribunal may be impeached on the grounds described in Section 334(a) of the Constitution.

If it is necessary to impeach the chairperson or any member of the Tribunal, then that shall be done so in accordance with the provisions prescribed in Section 302 of the Constitution. According to this Section, if the President wishes to impeach any member of the Tribunal, he shall submit his charge to the Speaker of Pyidaungsu Hluttaw. When the Speaker of the Pyidaungsu Hluttaw receives the charge of the President, they shall form an investigation body and cause the charge to be investigated in accordance with the law. In forming the investigation body, an equal number of representatives of the Pyithu Hluttaw and the Amyotha Hluttaw shall be included and any suitable member of the body be nominated as the chairperson of such body. The Speaker of the Pyidaungsu Hluttaw shall, upon receiving the findings of the investigations concerning the impeachment from the investigating body, present it to the Pyidaungsu Hluttaw. If a resolution is passed that the charge has been substantiated and the alleged person is unfit to continue serving as the chairperson or member of the Tribunal by two-thirds of the total number of the Pyidaungsu Hluttaw representatives, the Speaker of the Pyidaungsu Hluttaw shall present and report the said resolution to the President. On presentation of the report, the President shall proceed to remove the impeached person from office.

If the representatives of the Pyithu Hluttaw or the Amyotha Hluttaw wish to impeach, they are required to follow the impeachment provisions prescribed under Section 71 of the Constitution. According to this Section, their charge should be signed by not less than one-fourth of the total number of representatives of each Hluttaw and be submitted to the Head of the Hluttaw concerned. Action will only proceed if this charge is supported by not less than two-thirds of the total number of the Hluttaw concerned. If one Hluttaw supports the taking of action, the other Hluttaw shall form a body to investigate the charge. If the Hluttaw that investigates the charge resolves and reports that the charge made upon the chairperson or the member of the Tribunal has been substantiated and the person is unfit to continue serving as a chairperson or member of the Tribunal, the President shall proceed to remove the impeached person from his office.

In Myanmar, only one case of impeachment has been witnessed. After the Tribunal ruling on submission 1/2012, Amyotha Hluttaw representatives initiated the impeachment of members of the Tribunal based on the fact that they had breached provisions of the Constitution and they were unable to discharge their duties as assigned by the law. This led to resignations of the tribunal judges because the Hluttaw approved the impeachment. The combined Hluttaw then announced that the judgment of the Tribunal on submission 1/2012 was invalid. According to the Constitution, the Tribunal is the only judicial organization with the power to resolve constitutional disputes. The Tribunal's judgment being rejected by a vote of the Pyidaungsu Hluttaw implied that the Pyidaungsu Hluttaw can decide the constitutionality of the laws they make themselves.

4.3 Who Can Submit a Case on Issues of Constitutionality?

A constitutional matter may be directly submitted to the Tribunal by the

President of the Union, the Speaker of the Pyidaungsu Hluttaw, the Speaker of the Pyithu Hluttaw, the Speaker of Amyotha Hluttaw, the Chief Justice of the Union, and the Chairperson of the Union Election Commission to obtain a constitutional interpretation, resolution, or an opinion of the Tribunal pursuant to Section 325 of the Constitution. This provision is replicated in Section 13 of the Constitutional Tribunal of the Union Law.

In addition to those individuals, the Chief Minister of the Region or State, the Speaker of the Region or State Hluttaw, the Chairperson of the Self-Administered Division Leading Body or the Self-Administered Zone Leading Body, and at least 10% of all members of the Pyithu Hluttaw or Amyotha Hluttaw may submit matters to the Tribunal to obtain an interpretation, resolution, or opinion. Their submissions have to comply with the provisions of Section 326 of the Constitution and Section 14 of the Constitutional Tribunal of the Union Law.

Under Section 15 of the Constitutional Tribunal of the Union Law, individuals or institutions who are unable to submit their petition directly to the Tribunal, they can do it indirectly—through a state official such as the President of the Union or Speakers of Pyidaungsu Hluttaw, Pyithu Hluttaw, and Amyotha Hluttaw and others who have the right to submit such matters to the Tribunal directly. Therefore, a private individual cannot bring a case directly to the Tribunal.

4.4 Constitutional Review and International Human Rights Law

Constitutions usually follow to the fundamental standards of international law and human rights values. However, while governments implement the necessary laws to attain international recognition and acceptance, constitutions generally vary in their treatment of international law and international relations.

Although the right of citizens to apply for writs is a prerogative right guaranteed under Section 296(a) of the Constitution and Section 16(a) of the Union Judiciary Law, 2010, the Supreme Court has the authority to suspend applications for the issuance of writs in the state of emergency under Section 296(b) of the Constitution and Section 16(b) of the Union Judiciary Law, 2010. This is not in line with international human rights.

In Myanmar, international standards have constitutional effects or are directly applied as part of the legal processes. However, sometimes the national government focuses on basic domestic rights.

International treaties are subjects of constitutional review in most countries. On the contrary, in Myanmar, international treaties are not subjects of constitutional review. Only the Supreme Court of the Union has original jurisdiction on matters arising out of bilateral treaties concluded by the Union. This court also has jurisdiction over piracy offenses committed within the grounds or international waters or airspaces that violate international laws.[23]

The judges have to decide cases in accordance with the judicial principles mentioned in Section 19 of the Constitution and Section 3 of the Union Judiciary Law, 2010.

4.5 Matters that can be Reviewed by the Constitutional Tribunal of the Union

Only persons already mentioned in Sections 325 and 326 of the Constitution and Sections 13 and 14 of the Constitutional Tribunal of the Union Law can submit constitutional matters to the Tribunal; citizens cannot submit constitutional issues to the Tribunal. However, citizens are allowed to apply for writs to the Supreme Court under Section 296 of the Constitution and Section 16 of the Union Judiciary Law 2010. In Section 11(c) of the Union Judiciary Law, only the Supreme Court of the Union has original jurisdiction to hear and determine disputes among regions, states, and between a region and a state and between the Union Territory and a Region or a State, except in instances where such disputes are constitutional problems.[24] This means that judicial review is conferred on the Supreme Court. The Constitutional review is vested only in the Constitutional Tribunal.

The Constitution entrusts the Constitutional Tribunal with the power to settle disputes between the Union, regions, and self-administered areas, as well

---

[23] Section 11(a) and (d), the Union Judiciary Law, 2010.
[24] Section 11(c), Ibid.

as among them under Section 322(d). The Tribunal evaluates, through judicial proceedings, legislation and other governmental acts to ensure that they comply with the Constitution as stipulated under Section 322 of the Constitution. Therefore, the Tribunal is explicitly mandated to examine the constitutionality of law.

(1) Jurisdiction on Constitutional Interpretation

In Myanmar, according to Section 322(a) of the Constitution, the power to interpret the Constitution is conferred to the Constitutional Tribunal of the Union.

With regard to constitutional interpretation, the Constitutional Tribunal of the Union decided the issues presented in The Attorney-General of the Union, on behalf of the President of the Union v. 1. The Speaker, the Pyidaungsu Hluttaw, 2. The Speaker, the Pyithu Hluttaw, 3. The Speaker, and the Amyotha Hluttaw[25] on March 28, 2012.

The Attorney-General, on behalf of the President, presented a question relating to "Committees, Commissions, and Bodies formed by each Hluttaw." The issue was whether they should be regarded as "Union Level Organizations" or not. The definition of the term "Union Level Organization" is prescribed in Section 2(1) of the Law Relating to Pyidaungsu Hluttaw, Section 2(h) of the Law Relating to Pyithu Hluttaw, and Section 2(h) of the Law Relating to Amyotha Hluttaw as follows: "Union Level Organization means the Union Government, the National Defence and Security Council, the Financial Commission, the Supreme Court of the Union, the Constitutional Tribunal of the Union, the Union Election Commission, the Office of the Auditor General of the Union and the Union Civil Services Board formed under the Constitution and as well as the Committees, the Commissions and the bodies formed by Pyidaungsu Hluttaw, Pyithu Hluttaw, and Amyotha Hluttaw."

Although the term "Union Level Organization" is defined by the Laws Relating to the Hluttaws, the interpretation of the term is not present in the provisions of the Constitution. Therefore, to analyze the issues stated in the submission,

---

[25] Submission No. 1/2012.

some provisions of the Constitution needed to be scrutinized.

Sections 115 to 118 are concerned with the formation of the Pyithu Hluttaw Committees, Commissions, and Bodies while Sections 147–150 deal with the formation of the Amyotha Hluttaw Committees, Commissions, and Bodies.

Taking into consideration the expressions used in all the relevant sections, the term "Union Level Organization" means organizations formed under the Constitution directly and are different from the committees, commissions, and bodies formed by each Hluttaw.

After discussing on the above matters, the Tribunal also took into account the interpretation of Chapter IV of the Constitution under the heading of Legislature, which provides that "any of the Union Level Organizations formed under the Constitution" and "Organizations or Persons representing any of the Union Level Organization formed under the Constitution" shall be defined as "the Union Level Organizations or Persons appointed by the President with the approval of the Pyidaungsu Hluttaw. But Committees, Commissions, and Bodies formed by each Hluttaw shall be regarded only as organizations of Hluttaw."

Therefore, the Tribunal interpreted that "any of the Union Level Organizations formed under the Constitution" and "Organizations or persons representing any of the Union Level Organization formed under the Constitution" are the Union Level Organizations or Persons appointed by the President with the approval of the Pyidaungsu Hluttaw.

Based on all these reasons, the submission of the President was granted and "The status granted to Committees, Commissions, and Bodies formed by each Hluttaw as Union Level Organizations is unconstitutional."

The Hluttaw's members were outraged by this decision because they felt that the ruling was dropping the balance of power toward the executive by limiting the power of parliamentary committees to call and question government ministers. As a result, the Hluttaw impeached the entire Constitutional Tribunal of the Union, and the judges of the Constitutional Tribunal were forced to resign. In my point of view, the decision to impeach the entire court was a major setback for judicial independence under the Constitution. It appears that the executive and Constitutional Tribunal were operating within their rights and, as such, the legislature had no power to overrule the decisions of the Constitutional Tribunal, whose rulings are supposed to be "final and conclusive."[26]

Later, in January 2013, the Hluttaw amended the Constitutional Tribunal of the Union Law to secure greater legislative oversight of the appointment process. Section 12(i) of the Constitutional Tribunal of the Union Law provides that "the Tribunal's judges are required to report, in respect of the performance of their functions and duties, to the relevant President, or the Pyithu Hluttaw Speaker or Amyotha Hluttaw Speaker who nominated them." This provision seems to indicate that the Tribunal, which is a part of the judiciary, is not independent from the legislative and executive manipulation. Therefore, it can slant its balance of power and section 12 (i) of the Constitutional Tribunal of the Union Law is unconstitutional because the Constitutional Tribunal of the Union, which is a judicial organ, is to be under the executive and legislature. This issues stem from various areas within the Constitution; for instance, where the allocation of powers to the different branches of government is vague and shows a need for further Constitutional reform.

(2) Constitutional Review of Legislative Acts

In exercising constitutional review, the Constitutional Court and other equivalent bodies have the power to decide whether internal laws enacted by the legislature are constitutional or not. This scope of jurisdiction can also be found in judicial review.

In Myanmar, according to Section 322(b) of the Constitution, the Constitutional Tribunal has the power to vet whether the laws promulgated by the legislatures are in conformity with the Constitution or not.

On December 14, 2011, the Tribunal deiced the case of Dr. Aye Maung and 22 Representatives v. The Republic of the Union of Myanmar.[27]

---

[26] Section 23, the Constitutional Tribunal of Union Law.
[27] Submission No. 2/2011.

Dr. Aye Maung and 22 members of the Pyithu Hluttaw submitted a question on whether the term "Minister of the National Races Affairs" used in Section 5 of the Law of Emoluments, Allowances and Insignia for Representatives of the Region or State is included in the term of the "Ministers of the Region or State" or not.

The main issues of this case were whether the status of Ministers of the National Races Affairs is equal to that of the Ministers of the Region or State concerned and whether they are entitled to the emoluments, allowances, and insignia of office just like the Ministers of the Region or State.

The Tribunal held that Sections 262(a)(iv) and 262(e) of the Constitution define the "Minister of the National Races Affairs" as the "Minister of the Region or State" concerned. Consequently, Section 262(g)(ii) of the Constitution allows the President to assign duties to Hluttaw representatives who are Ministers of the Region or State, key among them being to perform the affairs of the National Races concerned. These provisions clearly give the Minister of the National Races Affairs and the other Ministers of the Region or State an equal status without any discrimination.

In the case of The Speaker of the Mon State Hluttaw v. The Republic of the Union of Myanmar Submission No. 3/2012,[28] which was decided on July 27, 2012, the following matters were submitted by the Speaker of the Mon State Hluttaw to the Constitutional Tribunal of the Union for interpretation:

- whether legislative power exercised by Mon State is or is not contrary to Section 446 of the Constitution;

- whether the existing laws that contradict Schedule Two, under Section 188 of the Constitution, still remain in force or not;

- whether the Region or State Hluttaw shall continue to exercise its legislative power until the laws that are inconsistent with the Constitution are repealed or amended.

The Pyidaungsu Hluttaw has the right to enact laws for the sectors prescribed

---

[28] Submission No. 3/2012.

in Schedule One of the Union Legislative list under Section 96 of the Constitution. Similarly, the Region or State Hluttaw has also the right to enact laws for the sectors prescribed in Schedule Two of the Region or State Legislative list under Section 188 of the Constitution.

Therefore, the exercise of its right to enact the Development Committees Law by the Mon State Hluttaw as a whole or in any part of the Mon State is permitted by the Constitution.

The Tribunal decided and interpreted that:

"where there are the laws and provisions contrary to or confused with the provisions contained in schedule two under section 188 of the Constitution, it shall be carried out after repeal and amendment under section 446 of the Constitution."

Enactment of laws and implementation of legislative powers permitted in Schedule Two shall be advised to exercise only after repealing or amending of the provisions of existing laws."

(3) Jurisdiction over Executive Acts

The Constitutional Court and other equivalent bodies are also mandated to decide the constitutionality of acts of central and local executive authorities. This power is exercised in both constitutional reviews and judicial reviews. However, in practice, this power is mostly exercised in constitutional reviews.

Under Section 322(c) of the Constitution, the power of vetting whether the measures of executive authorities of the Union, regions, states, and the self-administered areas are in conformity with the Constitution or not is conferred to the Constitutional Tribunal.

The Constitutional Tribunal of the Union of Myanmar has the power to decide constitutional disputes between the Union and a region, between the Union and a state, between a region and a state, among regions, among states, between a region or a state and a self-administered area, and among self-administered areas under Section 322(d) of the 2008 Constitution.

The authority to impeach the President and the Vice President of the State falls within the peculiar powers of constitutional review. This authority is not exercised through judicial review because the scope of judicial review is limited to political matters. Some countries that exercise constitutional review do not grant this power of impeachment to constitutional courts or other equivalent bodies. For example, the Republic of the Union of Myanmar.

In The Chief Justice of the Union v. Ministry of Home Affairs,[29] a case that was decided on July 14, 2011, the Chief Justice of the Union Supreme Court, as an applicant, submitted to the Constitutional Tribunal a matter questioning the legality of conferring first class judicial powers to sub-township administrative officers, as requested by the Ministry of Home Affairs (the defendant in this case).

Upon receiving the request, the Chief Justice of the Union Supreme Court referred this case to the Tribunal to vet the constitutionality of the appointment of the sub-township administrative officers as judicial officers under Section 293 and Section 317 of the Constitution; conferring the first class power of magistrates under Section 32(1)(a) of the Criminal Procedure Code to the sub-township administrative officers and also giving magistrates powers to sit in a trial summary under Section 260 of the Criminal Procedure Code; and finally appointing sub-township administrative officers as juvenile judges and empowering them to try juvenile cases under Section 40(a) of the Child Law, 1993.

The Constitutional Tribunal held that provisions of the Constitution clearly stipulate that the legislative power, the executive power, and the judicial power of the Union shall be separately exercised. The judicial power granted to courts and judges are clearly prescribed in the Constitution. Therefore, the exercise of such judicial power is permitted only to those judges who are empowered by the Constitution.

The conferring of the judicial power to administrative officers of the General Administration Department of the Ministry of Home Affairs was, therefore, not in conformity with the Constitution.

---

[29] Submission No. 1/2011.

(4) Jurisdiction over Political Parties and Elections

In Myanmar, the Constitutional Tribunal does not interfere in election cases and dissolution of political parties. It only exercises its power of constitutional review according to Section 322 of the Constitution without interfering with the powers of the Union Election Commission.

In U Aung Kyi Nyunt, a member of the Amyotha Hluttaw, and other 26 members of the Amyotha Hluttaw[30] case, which was decided on February 27, 2015, the applicants submitted a question of the constitutionality of the proportional representation (PR) system for the election of Ayotha Hluttaw.

First, the law proposed for the adoption of the PR System in the Amyotha Hluttaw had not been enacted. Second, the decision could not be settled before the Pyithu Hluttaw and Pyidaungsu Hluttaw. Therefore, the Tribunal had the power to review the constitutionality of the law once the Bill was passed into law.

Consequently, it is clear that the Tribunal has the power to review only the enacted laws and not bills.

---

[30] Submission No. 5/2014.

Chapter 8

USE OF COMMON TOPIC METHOD TO PROMOTE INCLUSIVE LEGAL EDUCATION:

Extending Topics from Private to Public Law

Hiroshi Matsuo*

(Keio University)

The study of the private law ... depends upon a detailed analysis of the uses and limits of the autonomy principle. ... The law of eminent domain illustrates par excellence the social limitations upon the private rights of ownership. The matter is evident from the text of the takings clause of the Constitution, which says, "Nor shall private property be taken for public use, without just compensation."

There is no internal limitation on the scope of the takings clause. As we move from simple to complex cases, we move down the continuum from private to public law. There is no clean break on that continuum between disputes with two parties and those with two hundred million. Private law and public law no longer fall into separate domains. The modern view is that private law gets submerged in the rush to public law. My position is exactly the reverse: to make sense of the system, we must "go public" with private law. The rules of public law make sense only if they can be "reduced" to propositions that are understandable in private-law terms. ...

---

* Professor, Keio University Law School; Director, Keio Institute for Global Law and Development (KEIGLAD).

Or so I thought. The case law, however, tells a very different story. ... Even a cursory examination of its [the Supreme Court's] decisions shows a radical disjunction between the private and the public faces of the law. In instance after instance the Court has held state controls to be compatible with the rights of private property. The state can now rise above the rights of the persons whom it represents; it is allowed to assert novel rights that it cannot derive from the persons whom it benefits. Private property once may have been conceived as a barrier to government power, but today that barrier is easily overcome, almost for the asking.[1]

1. Introduction

The topics in the previous trial of common topic method for the international legal education program were selected from private law issues on which comparative research on the basic principles of property law, contract law, tort law, family law and succession law could be conducted[2]. The present trial of common topic method intends to extend the topic scope from the private to the public law field so as to deepen the understanding of private law principles associated with the guarantee of private autonomy and the protection of private property rights and consider their relationships with public law.

In this context, the protection of private property in the procedure of public takings (compulsory purchase or expropriation of private property by the government agency for the promotion of public interest) could be a topic in which stu-

---

[1] Richard Epstein and Richard Allen Epstein, *Takings : Private Property and the Power of Eminent Domain*, Harvard University Press, 1985, pp. ix-x.

[2] Hiroshi Matsuo, "Use of Common Topics to Improve Comparative Law and Legal Education in Asia", in: KEIGLAD (ed.), *How Civil Law Is Taught in Asian Universities* (Program for Asian Global Legal Professions [PAGLEP] Series III), Keio University Press, 2019, pp. 243–254. As for the application of Japanese law, Vietnamese law, Cambodian law, Lao law, Thai law, and Myanmar law to the common topics, see, ibid., pp. 255–309.

dents could compare the concept of private property and how it can be restricted for the public project, the scope of its protection in the expropriation process, and the determination of just compensation for takings. They will find that there are variations in the treatment of these issues because of different interpretation of what is private property right in relation to state power (eminent domain).

Some may think that the state has an original property right that is prior over the private property of the citizen so that the power of expropriation shall be drawn from that original property right[3]. Others may believe that the power of public takings originates in the citizens' private property rights which have been trusted to the state; therefore, the exercise of the takings power and the restriction of private property right must be explained using propositions that are able to be translated into private law terms[4]. Thus the protection of private property right of a citizen provided by private law is linked with the exercise of expropriation power of a state provided by public law in the topic of public takings. This link between private and public law seems to be based on the fundamental understanding of the state-citizen relationship in each country. We can ask the students: how is the state thought to be special over a private person in your country?

By harnessing comparative research and encouraging discussion on the public takings topic, students will better understand the similarities and differences between their own country and other countries in terms of the provisions of law on public takings, the interpretation of these provisions, the role of precedents

---

[3] Hobbes admits that "All private Estates of land proceed originally from the arbitrary Distribution of the Sovereign", and "Propriety of a Subject excludes not the Dominion of the Sovereign, but only of another Subject" (Thomas Hobbes, *Leviathan*, 1651, Part 2, Chapter 24, p. 128). He also puts it: "Propriety", that is, "the whole power of prescribing the Rules, whereby every man may know, what Goods he may enjoy, and what Actions he may do, without being molested by any of his fellow Subjects", "is annexed to the Sovereignty". "For before constitution of Sovereign Power ... all men had right to all things, which necessarily caused War: and therefore this Propriety, being necessary to Peace, and depending on Sovereign Power, is the Act of that Power, in order to the public peace" (ibid., Part 2, Chapter 18, p. 91).

[4] Epstein, op. cit. (note 1), p. ix.

(case laws), and the effectiveness of law to solve the conflicts over the expropriation and compensation for it. The common topic method allows students and teachers to participate in inclusive discussions that go beyond the differences of the content of law, the role of law in society, and the relationship between the state and the people in each country. Through this type of inclusive forum, participants may identify the common principles which could explain the reasons for different provisions of law in accordance with the legal development in each country.

The public takings topic may interest not only students and teachers but also government officials, public agencies, business people, lawyers, activists, and citizens who are or will be actually involved in the expropriation for public projects. If they participate in this forum as mentioned above, discussions should become more inclusive, and various aspects exchanged among participants could lead to the development of a consistent and comprehensive theory of property[5]. It will be a fruitful outcome of the common topic method for the promotion of inclusive legal education.

2. Common Topic from Public Law Issues

2.1 Case

A, the Road Agency, made a plan to construct a thirty kilometer highway connecting City P and City Q with the aim of improving transportation between these cities and promoting industrial development (see [Figure 1]).

B owns a piece of land (300 m²) on which there is a three-story house in which he lives with his wife and a child. One room of the house is rented to M for USD 1000 per month. B's land is located within the highway project area.

C owns a piece of land (1000 m²) on which ten possessors without title (N1 to

---

[5] As for the analysis of takings and compensation from the theory of property, see Stephen R. Munzer, *A Theory of Property*, Cambridge University Press, pp. 442–469.

[Figure 1] Case

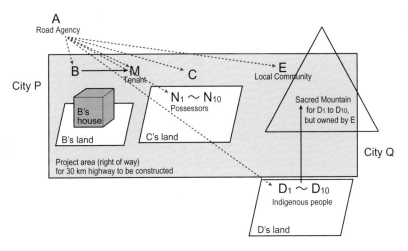

N10) have lived for ten years. C's land is located within the highway project area.

D1 to D10 (ten people) are a group of indigenous people who own land and houses very close to the highway project area. There is a small sacred mountain near their houses, which is important to their traditional beliefs. They pray every day facing the direction of that mountain. It is owned by local community E to which D1 to D 10 belong. A negotiated with E and acquired the rights to mountain because it is within the highway project area as A plans to build a tunnel through the mountain as part of the highway construction, which will change the shape of the sacred mountain for D1 to D10.

2.2 Questions

2.2.1 [Question 1]

A asked B to sell B's land and B agreed. What compensation should be given to B? What compensation should be given to M?

2.2.2 [Question 2]

A asked C to sell C's land and C agreed. However, N1 to N10 refuse to vacate

C's land. What compensation should be given to C? What measures can A take to promote the project and remove N1 to N10 from C's land? Does A need compensate N1 to N10 if they agree or are forced to leave C's land?

2.2.3 [Question 3]

D1 to D10 do not agree with A's plan to build a tunnel through the mountain. What claims can they make against A to these changes? What measures can A take to ensure the project goes ahead in the face of the opposition by D1 to D10? Does A need to compensate D1 to D10?

2.3 Discussion Points

2.3.1 For [Question 1]

(1) Compensation for Land and Building

[Question 1] is focused on the basic takings process rules and the methods for and calculation of adequate compensation. A voluntary agreement between the public agency and the rights holder may be concluded before the takings. The takings process begins when there is a failure to agree between the public agency and the rights holder.

The first question is concerned with the methods for and the calculation of compensation to be agreed between the public agency and the rights holder as well as the compulsory purchase procedure and compensation to be paid by the public agency to the rights holder.

The question is divided into two smaller questions: how to calculate the compensation for B's land and how to calculate the compensation for B's house. For both questions the answers will depend on the land and building treatment in each jurisdiction, that is, whether the land and the building on it are an immovable property or separate properties.

(a) If B's building is integrated into B's land they are seen as a set of immovable property and the compensation is calculated based on the set value for both the land and the building.

(b) If they are classified as separate properties, B will be asked to remove the

building to another appropriate place by an appropriate method and the compensation calculated based on the value of the land without any building on it plus
the expense for changing the place of the building.

(2) Compensation for the Interest of the Tenant in the House

[Question 1] also asks about the compensation for the tenant in the house. Is
it necessary to compensate M? If so, how should the compensation be calculated?

M has no legal right to the land but only has a right to the house. How can
compensation for M be justified from the viewpoint of "just" compensation for
the property taken?

2.3.2 For [Question 2]

[Question 2] is about the compensation for C's land and the need to compensate the interest of the possessors N1 to N 10, none of whom have any formal
legal title to the land to be taken.

The question regarding the method and calculation of the compensation for C
is similar to that for B's land in [Question 1] and is resolved based on the value of
C's land.

The problem is whether it is necessary for A to compensate N1 to N10 as this
may depend on the historical background, why they are occupying the land, and
how long they have continued to occupy it.

Depending on the law provisions in each jurisdiction, it would be difficult for
N1 to N10 to claim ownership even if they had been there for ten years because
this land belongs to C and C might not have known that N1 to N10 had occupied
C's land.

However, N1 to N10 may claim that their ancestors were the original owners
of the land and they had succeeded their title to the land even though they were
unable to prove this with any written documents or registration; therefore, they
took C to court, but failed.

If it is recognized that the interests of N1 to N10 should be protected to a
certain extent because of the historical occupation, the question is what "just"

compensation would be from the public takings viewpoint; that is, what is the relationship between the public policy to remove N1 to N10 from the project site and just compensation for property taken.

2.3.3 For [Question 3]

(1) The Rights of Indigenous People

In [Question 3], A has to negotiate with E to purchase the ownership of a certain area in a mountain and establish the right to use another area to maintain the tunnel, and must compensate E for the acquisition of those rights.

The problem is whether A also needs to negotiate with D1 to D10, the indigenous people living near the mountain, regarding the tunnel construction through the mountain and whether A should provide them with any compensation. D1 to D10 own their land and houses, and while being close to the project site, they are not within its boundaries. Therefore, what rights do they have over the sacred mountain within the project area for their traditional worship. The interest that D1 to D10 have in this mountain is not an object of ownership, and there is no right to use, profit from, or possess the land. If it is not a property right, is it a personality right, that is, the right of the individual, or is it the indigenous people's collective right to practice their cultural rights? If they have no legal rights to the mountain or the project area under the national legal system, how can their interests be considered in the public takings. If their interests are protected by rights based on the act, customary law, or case law, the content and effect of these rights must be confirmed.

Extending from this question is the process A may need to follow to promote a project that affects the interests of the indigenous people. For instance, does the principle of Free, Prior and Informed Consent (FPIC hereafter)[6] apply to this case, and if it does, how can it be treated and implemented by the project agency and the court within the national legal system.

---

[6] As for the FPIC, see United Nations Declaration on the Rights of Indigenous Peoples, Resolution adopted by the General Assembly on 13 September 2007, U. N. Doc. A/RES/61/295.

Finally, it is necessary to ask whether compensation is needed for D1 to D10, and if so, how could this be given to ensure the interests of the indigenous people.

(2) A Related Case for Reference

Related to [Question 3], there was a case known as "Nibutani Dam Case" in Japan[7]. In 1978, the Minister of Construction revised a river management plan and decided to construct two dams on the Saru River in Hokkaido, in the northern part of Japan, to provide water and electricity for a planned industrial development zone "Tomakomai Tobu" located on the Pacific coast and to local residents in the Nibutani region, for which a basic construction plan was developed in 1983. In 1984, the Hokkaido Development Agency (HDA hereafter), a local branch of the Ministry of Construction, began purchasing the necessary land for the project. About one third of the landowners residing on the Nibutani Dam construction project site were Ainu, the indigenous people living in the northern regions in Japan. However, the HDA could not agree with two of the Ainu residents, X1 and X2 (plaintiffs), on the purchase of their land. In April 1986, the HDA applied for project recognition from the Minister of Construction, which was a necessary requirement for land expropriation based on the Land Expropriation Law, which was granted in December 1986. In response to the land expropriation application, in November 1987, the Hokkaido Land Expropriation Committee (defendant, HLEC hereafter) made a decision to recognize the HDA expropriation and to order X1 and X2 to vacate their land in February 1989. X1 and X2 did not accept the decision and requested the Minister of Construction review the HLEC's decision in March 1989, even though the dam construction had started in September 1986. As the Minister of Construction rejected their request for the review of the HLEC's decision, X1 and X3 (the son of X2 who died in 1992) took the case to the Sapporo District Court in 1993 seeking a revocation

---

[7] Kayano et al. v. Hokkaido Expropriation Committee (the Nibutani Dam Decision), March 27, 1997, *Hanrei Jiho* 1598–33; *Hanrei Times* 938–75 (translated by Mark A. Levin, International Legal Material, 38–397, 1999; Kaori Tahara, "Asia & Pacific: Nibutani Dam Case", [1999] *IndigLawB* 70, (1999) 4 (23) *Indigenous Law Bulletin* 18.

of the HLEC's decision.

At the trial, X1 and X3 claimed that the dam construction site included sacred areas for the Ainu, such as the places for Cip-sanke (launching ceremony), Ci-nomi-sir (oracle) and Casi (fort) and alleged that the HDA had not accounted for the losses to Ainu culture.

The District Court of Sapporo held that: (a) the HLEC's decisions that recognized the expropriation and the vacation of the Ainu land were illegal and that it was possible to rescind those decisions under the Land Expropriation Law; (b) the Ainu are the indigenous people of Hokkaido[8] and have the right to the pursuit of happiness and the right to enjoy their own culture, which are guaranteed by Art. 13 of the Constitution of Japan and Art. 27 of the International Covenant on Civil and Political Rights (ICCPR hereafter) that shall be faithfully observed by the government under Art. 98 (2) in the Constitution of Japan. However, (c) the court held that while the HLEC's decisions were illegal, it was in the public interest not to rescind the decisions by the HLEC because the dam was already complete and was being used to store water[9]. The decision of the District Court of Sapporo was final because neither party filed an appeal to the High Court.

Different from D1 to D10 in Common Topic Case (above 2.1), X1 and X2 in this case owned their land within the project area. However, the decision which recognized the right to enjoy own culture will apply to both cases. In the background to this conflict was the Japanese invasion of Hokkaido Island by the Meiji government and the compulsory application of Japanese law to the Ainu homeland in the early years of the Meiji Restoration, which started in 1868. Since that time, the Japanese government has tried to assimilate the Ainu into Japanese

---

[8] According to the court decision, indigenous peoples were defined as social groups who have lived in a region prior to colonization and who have subsequently maintained their distinct culture and identity.

[9] The judgment in which the court recognizes the plaintiff's claim for confirming the illegality of the decisions by the defendant, however, rejects the claim for rescinding the decisions if it is necessary or unavoidable for the public interest is called "Jijo Hanketsu" (judgment by taking into consideration of the circumstances) in Japanese.

society and to take control of Hokkaido Island's land and natural resources. While this is a Japanese case, similar conflicts may have occurred in in other countries because of land confiscation due to the centralization of political power and the establishment of sovereignty. Therefore, this problem could be treated as a kind of takings and compensation problem, even though it was before the establishment of an integrated state legal system.

3. Conclusion

3.1 The Differences between Private and Public Law in the Compensation Issue

From the analysis of the answers to the questions above it is evident that the compensation for takings provided by public law (such as the constitutional guarantee of private property and just compensation for public use and land appropriation law) and the compensation for damages provided by private law (such as the provisions of civil code and other special laws) are not the same[10].

First, the compensation for takings is for losses caused by lawful actions without fault of the government and public agencies, and the compensation for damages is for illegal actions resulting from intention, negligence or fault of any actors including the government and public agencies.

Second, the scope for the compensation for takings does not always include mental loss[11], while that for damage compensation caused by tortious action does cover mental damage[12].

Third, the scope for compensation for takings does not always include the economic loss suffered by the holder of the private property taken, while that

---

[10] The following summary is based on: Hiroshi Matsuo, *Zaisanken-no-hosho-to-sonshitsu-hosho-no-hori [A Theory of Property Rights and Compensation for Takings]*, Taisei-shuppan-sha, 2011, pp. 19–20.

[11] Supreme Court Decision, January 27, 1981, Minshu 35–1–35.

[12] As for the Japanese law, for instance, Sec. 710 Civil Code of Japan.

for damage compensation caused by tortious action may include such economic losses if foreseeable by the wrongdoer.

Fourth, compensation for takings may be challenged by administrative procedure, while compensation for damages caused by tortious action is litigated according to civil procedure.

Although these differences are not always present in all jurisdictions, it would be interesting to examine the reasons for any differences between the public and private compensation laws in some jurisdictions. One of the possible reasons for the differences may be that the compensation for takings is not the *atonement* for damages to be paid to the victim of illegal and tortious action by the wrongdoer[13], but the *reallocation* of the interests from the increased benefits by the public project in consideration of the contribution by the related persons to that project[14]; that is, as it involves coordinating the benefits and losses arising from the public project, in some cases the private property rights holders may have to endure loss with the other rights holders[15]. In this context, the private property rights holder cannot be seen as a *victim* of illegal and tortious action but as a *participant* in a public project that aims to increase the sum of interest for all citizens.

3.2 The Ultimate Question to Be Sought Using the Common Topic Method

An inquiry into the reasons for the differences between compensation for loss caused by the public law takings and compensation for damages caused by illegal and tortious actions in private law and a recognition of the creation of in-

---

[13] In this case, the corrective justice shall be applied to solve the problem.

[14] In this case, the corrective justice should not be applied because the problem is different from the compensation for damages due to the illegal and tortious action, but another justice to reallocate benefits and losses to be caused by the public projects among the citizen (so to speak the reallocative justice) shall be applied to solve the question. Matsuo, op. cit. (note 10), pp. 38–40.

[15] Matsuo, op. cit. (note 10), pp. 14–15, pp. 22–23.

terests in public projects would lead to further inquiries regarding the reason for the state to be the agent for public projects, which would lead to the fundamental question: "What are the reasons for the formation of the state?"[16]

Even if the state is able to increase the sum of private interest in society, is it the result of the coordination of the individuals' private property that existed before the formation of the state? If so, by the provisions of the law, any surpluses generated by the public project should be divided between the individuals in accordance with the proportion of their contributions with none being left to the state[17]. Or, does the state provide individuals with private property through the detailed legal provisions that regulate the acquisition, protection, and disposition of the property? If so, there may be a room for the state to reserve a certain portion of the surplus gained from the public project to redistribute and ensure the effective implementation of the public project. In other words, does the individual's right of private property create the law or does the law create the individual's right of private property? However, this appears to be a chicken and egg problem and both extremes are a little remote from reality. On the one hand, if the rights of citizens are articulated by the provisions of law, they can be more certainly and more effectively implemented. On the other hand, the right could be a potential source of a new law and could give the government the power to develop new rules to protect it[18], because rights are the principles that guide the development of new laws, and both the legislature and the court rely on the existence of rights to justify the development of new rules to protect these rights.

This question is closely related with another fundamental question as to what the rule of law means when guaranteeing the right of private property against public takings. If the formal definition of the rule of law (the rule-book conception or thin conception of the rule of law) is followed, the legality of the takings must conform with formal law provisions, and if the substantive definition (the

---

[16] Epstein, op. cit. (note 1), p. 3.

[17] Epstein, op. cit. (note 1), p. 5.

[18] Joseph Raz, *The Concept of a Legal System: An Introduction to the Theory of a Legal System*, Second Edition, Oxford University Press, 1980, p. 226.

rights conception or thick conception of the rule of law) is followed, the right-eousness of the takings and compensation must be reviewed by considering whether the formal law content corresponds to the substantive justice provided by the substantive rights[19]. However, here again it is necessary to avoid extreme understanding and seek to foster an overarching conception by introducing a dynamic, extensive concept for the rule of law[20].

3.3 The Necessity of Inclusive Legal Education Using the Common Topic Method

To avoid any extreme interpretations of the formation and existence of the state and determine the relationship between private property rights and the law, it is necessary to ensure that legal education should become more inclusive by using common topic method as this allows students, teachers, lawyers, government officials (judges, prosecutors, etc.), business people and people from different countries to more easily understand the diversity of law provisions associated with private property rights and interpretations of them and conceptions of the state. A more inclusive legal education can foster greater legal cooperation, and provide richer opportunities to exchange views and draw the common principles of law which can be flexibly applied to the unique contexts of each country in the dynamic legal development process (see [Figure 2])[21].

---

[19] Ronald Dworkin, *A Matter of Principle*, Harvard University Press, 1985, pp. 11–14; Randall Peerenboom, "Varieties of Rule of Law: An introduction and provisional conclusion," in: Randall Peernboom (ed.), *Asian Discourse of Rule of Law: Theories and implementation of rule of law in twelve Asian countries, France and the U. S.*, Routledge Curzon, pp. 2–5.

[20] As for the conception of the rule of law as a multi-layered, step-by-step promoted, and dynamically changing legal system, see Hiroshi Matsuo, "Let the Rule of Law be Flexible to Attain Good Governance," in: Per Bergling, Jenny Ederlöf and Veronica L. Taylor (eds.), *Rule of Law Promotion: Global Perspectives, Local Applications*, Iustus, Uppsala, 2009, pp. 41–56. See also Hiroshi Matsuo, "The Rule of Law and Economic Development: A Cause or a Result?," in: Yoshiharu Matsuura (ed.), *The Role of Law in Development: Past, Present and Future*, CALE Books 2, Nagoya University, pp. 59–70.

[21] Matsuo, op. cit. (note. 2), p. 254.

[Figure 2] Toward the Inclusive Legal Education

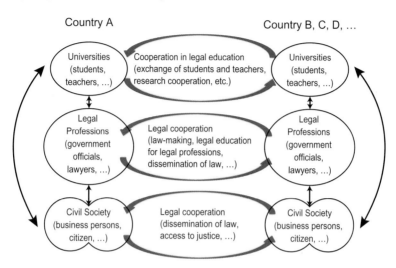

3.4 Application of the Common Topic Method

The common topic method using public law issues was implemented at an international seminar at Hanoi Law University on 13 September in 2019, at which law students from Vietnam, Laos, Cambodia, Thailand, Myanmar and Japan participated and gave presentations to answer the above questions by applying their own national laws, and had discussions in relation to them. The outcomes of the common topic application is reported in the following Chapter[22].

---

[22] See Hitomi Fukasawa, "From the Law Classroom in Asian Universities: A Short Report on the Collaboration Program in Vietnam", pp. 151–163 below.

Chapter 9

FROM THE LAW CLASSROOM IN ASIAN UNIVERSITIES:

A Short Report on the Collaboration Program in Vietnam

Hitomi Fukasawa*

(Keio University)

1. Introduction

From September 9 to 14, 2019, Keio University Law School (KLS: Tokyo Japan) conducted a multilateral Collaboration Law Study Program in Hanoi, Vietnam with KLS partner universities from Mekong region countries, Vietnam, Cambodia, Laos, Thailand, and Myanmar. The program consisted of (a) lectures about public law, especially on the constitutional law in each country, (b) presentations on common case topics by students, and (c) a site visit to the National Assembly of Vietnam. 36 students participated and 10 teachers took part in the program.

KLS began the Collaboration Law Study Program in 2017 in Mekong region countries. It has organized bilateral study programs with the Vietnam National University of Economics and Law (UEL: Ho Chi Minh City, Vietnam), the Pannasastra University of Cambodia, the Faculty of Law and Public Administration (PUC-FLPA: Phnom Penh Cambodia)[1], the Thammasat University Faculty of

---

* Ph.D. candidate, Keio University Graduate School of Law. Researcher, Keio University Law School Instute Global Law and Development (KEIGLAD).

[1] Hiroshi Matsuo=Hitomi Fukasawa, From Law Class Rooms in Asian Universities: Short Report on the Collaboration Program in Vietnam and Cambodia, KEIGLAD eds. *Compar-*

Law (TU: Bangkok, Thailand)[2], and the National University of Laos Faculty of Law and Political Science (NUOL: Vientiane, Laos). In addition to these bilateral study programs, it held a multilateral study program in Hanoi from 2018 with Hanoi Law University (HLU: Hanoi, Vietnam). The 2019 program was the second multilateral program for KLS.

Since the beginning of the Collaboration Law Study Program, KLS assigned a case called a "common topic." Each common topic consists of a legal case and questions. Students need to prepare a presentation about how the case will be solved by applying their home country laws before they join the program. During the program, students present their presentations and discuss them with participants from other countries.

The common topic provides a forum where students from different countries can discuss the similarities and differences in law about a particular topic from a comparative law perspective. Students learn about foreign laws and the variety of solutions to their particular topic, the principles underpinning the topic, the method of legal interpretation, the variety of sources of law, the role of precedents (case law), the possible changes to the law during the development stages of each country, and the possibility of legal reform in their home countries.

In this report, I introduce the 2019 Collaboration Law Study Program activities by focusing on student presentations. By reviewing presentations and discussions in the classroom, the report attempts to improve law education and its methodology in Asian universities.

---

ative Legal Education from Asian Perspective, Keio University Press (2017) pp. 157–174. Hitomi Fukasawa, From Law Class Rooms in Asian Universities: Short Report on the Collaboration Program in Cambodia in 2018, KEIGLAD eds. *How Civil Law Is Taught in Asian Universities*, Keio University Press (2019) pp. 313–329.

[2] Hiroshi Matsuo=Hitomi Fukasawa, From Law Classrooms in Asian Universities: Short Report on the Collaboration Program in Thailand, KEIGLAD eds. *Challenging for Studying Law Abroad in the Asian Region*, Keio University Press (2018) pp. 169–189.

2. Presentation and Discussion of the Common Topic

2.1 Overview

The common topic (pp. 135–149) was used in the 2019 program. All participants had a legal education background but had different learning histories. The
youngest student was a third-grade bachelor student and the oldest student was
enrolled in a judicial doctorate course. Students divided into seven groups based
on country and regions. There were seven groups from Hanoi, Ho Chi Minh
City, Cambodia, Laos, Thailand, Myanmar, and Japan. The common topic was
assigned one month before the program began. Each group was allocated 15 minutes for their presentation. The group discussion was around two hours.

2.2 Students Presentation and Discussion

Each group presented an explanation of how the common topic case was
solved by applying their country's national law. This chapter discussed how students answered three questions, their similarities, and differences.

2.2.1 Compensation to land and house owners, a tenant, and possessors

All groups concluded that B, the land and house owner, and C, the landowner
would be compensated for land acquisition from developer A. However, different
approaches to solutions were presented.

All presenters' countries had established rules on land expropriation to protect
land ownership. For example, Myanmar's Land Acquisition Act (1894) stipulates
compensation for land expropriation[3]. Similar laws exist in Cambodia[4], Thailand[5],

---

[3] Online Burma/Myanmar Library, *Land Acquisition Act (1894)*, https://www.burmalibrary.
org/docs23/1947-Burma_land_acquisition_manual-tu.pdf (Last accessed on January 6th 2020).
[4] World Bank, *Law on Expropriation*, https://ppp.worldbank.org/public-private-partnership/
sites/ppp.worldbank.org/files/documents/Cambodia_Law-on-Expropriation-%282010%29.
pdf (Last accessed on January 6th 2020).
[5] Thai Land Law Online, *Thai Land Law Act*, https://www.thailandlawonline.com/thai-real-
estate-law/thai-land-law-land-code-act (Last accessed on January 6th 2020).

The presentation
by Thai students

and Japan[6]. The socialist countries of Vietnam and Laos do not recognize private land ownership, yet have granted compensation rules for land use rights under existing Land Law[7].

Compensation for land and real estate is guaranteed in all countries although the method used to calculate house value was different. All countries except Myanmar calculated land and building prices separately and set a total price for compensation. Myanmar, on the other hand, includes the value of buildings in the price of land. This is because Myanmar civil law treats a building as a property attached to the land.

Regarding compensation to the tenant, M, all presenters explained that he should be protected, and would receive compensation; however, different approaches were adopted.

One approach stipulated that M should receive compensation money from

[6] Japanese Law Translation, *Expropriation of Land Act*, http://www.japaneselawtranslation.go.jp/law/detail/?id=3255&vm=04&re=01 (Last accessed on January 6th 2020).

[7] Thu Vien Phap Luat, *Land Law No. 45/2013/QH13*, https://thuvienphapluat.vn/van-ban/bat-dong-san/Luat-dat-dai-2013-215836.aspx (Last Accessed on January 6th 2020).

the land and house owner B. This view tries to protect the rights of the tenant through the contractual liability of a lessor. Team Vietnam, Laos and Myanmar adopted this approach.

Another method argued that developer A should pay compensation money directly to M. Cambodia, Thailand, and Japan adopted this provision.

In contrast to landowners, no countries had legal rules for compensating possessors without land titles. Students from Cambodia, Laos, Thailand, and Japan discussed the possibility of prescription. However, prescription was not recognized because it does not fulfill the requirements of any country.

2.2.2 Compensation for the cultural right of indigenous people

Various views on the protection of the cultural rights of ethnic minorities to their sacred mountain were discussed.

Cambodia and Thailand attempted to protect the right of indigenous people through legislation.

In Thailand, indigenous people, D1 to D10's rights to the sacred mountain may be protected by the Constitution. The Thai Constitution section 43 guarantees that a person and a community have the right to conserve, revive or promote wisdom, arts, culture, tradition and good customs at both local and national levels[8]. Section 43 paragraph (3) stipulates that a person and a community have the right to sign a joint petition to propose recommendations to a State agency to carry out any action deemed beneficial to the people, or the community, or refrain from any act which will affect their right to live in peace. The State has a duty to promote these rights which are guaranteed by section 43[9]. One discussion room explored whether indigenous people D1 to D10 are "a community" or not. If they were, they could sue developer A for stopping construction on the mountain at the Thai Constitutional Court. Although Thai citizens posses measures

---

[8] The Thai Constitution Section 43, http://constitutionnet.org/sites/default/files/2017-05/CONSTITUTION+OF+THE+KINGDOM+OF+THAILAND+(B.E.+2560+(2017)).pdf (Last accessed on January 6th, 2020).

[9] *Ibid*, Section 57.

that enable them to oppose a project, it is difficult to win a case. Thai students introduced an actual community eviction case that occurred in the Mahakan area in Bangkok for more than 20 years[10]. The city began a park construction project in Mahakan and issued an eviction order to residents living in the area. However, citizens opposed the project because it would damage community history and traditional wooden constructions, and claimed the right to live on the project site. However, the project was approved, and finally, 70% of residents were moved to other areas.

Thailand tries to protect the right of ethnic minorities group throughout the interpretation of its Constitution and court procedure. Meanwhile, Cambodian legislators have tried to protect the right of indigenous people more directly.

Cambodian Land Law articles 23 to 28 refer to the rights of indigenous people[11]. Article 23 defines "indigenous people" and article 28 guarantees indigenous people's community ownership of immovable property. However, the common topic was not the protection of ethnic groups' community ownership, because D1 to D10 did not own the mountain, but had just requested the protection of their cultural rights. Students concluded that Land Law could not be applied to the common topic case. Negotiations to reduce the project's environmental impact on the mountain may be one solution because no legislation protects cultural rights alone.

Neither Vietnam, Laos nor Myanmar law mentions "the rights of indigenous people" or "the protection of cultural rights." However, those countries students pointed out that each administration had an obligation to consider cultural values and impacts when granting a developer permission to construct.

---

[10] Rina Chandran, "Ancient fort community in Bangkok loses 25-year battle against bulldozers", *Reuters*, May 4th, 2018, https://www.reuters.com/article/us-thailand-landrights-property/ancient-fort-community-in-bangkok-loses-25-year-battle-against-bulldozers-idUSKBN1I5005 (Last accessed on January 6th, 2019).

[11] Unofficial English translation is available from WTO, *Land Law*, https://www.wto.org/english/thewto_e/acc_e/khm_e/WTACCKHM5_LEG_1.pdf (Last accessed on January 6th, 2020).

In Vietnam, Land Law stipulates some special procedures for developing land which has cultural and historical value (article 158).

Myanmar students explained that rather than legal protection due to cultural rights, indigenous people's rights may be protected by a decision making process in the Assembly. In Myanmar, when developments may affect the environment, tradition, and historical sites, the Assembly of the Union, *Pyidaungsu Hluttaw* decides on development project approval.

Lao students introduced the City Pillar Shrine case where the construction area for Vientiane No. 1 road was changed due to the discovery of relics[12].

While many countries considered the protection of ethnic minorities rights through policy-making decisions, Japanese students considered whether their rights could be protected using administrative and civil litigation. They examined the possibility of (1) action to revoke permission to construct on the mountain based on their cultural right, and (2) an injunction against construction due to property or personal rights of indigenous people. However, the students concluded that such actions would not be recognized by a court. This is because ethnic minorities do not own the mountain and it remains debatable whether a cultural right is guaranteed as a personal right in Japan.

Thus, as introduced above, students attempted to protect the cultural rights of indigenous people using various approaches. However, no clear remedies which led to the direct protection of cultural rights were identified.

2.2.3 Discussion

The student discussion was facilitated by the professor who suggested the common topic. The discussion points were (1) how to evaluate land and house prices, (2) how a tenant gets compensation, (3) compensation for possessors without land titles, and (4) compensation for cultural rights.

---

[12] For more details, see JICA "The project for the improvement of the Vientiane No. 1 Road", pp. 9–10 (2011), https://www2.jica.go.jp/ja/evaluation/pdf/2011_0603900_4_f.pdf (Last accessed on January 7th 2020).

(1) Evaluation of land and house prices

Except for Vietnam and Laos, all countries evaluated land prices using market prices. The socialist countries of Vietnam and Laos decide compensation for land using a land price list issued by a government. City and town areas are zoned in the list and determine the price of land in each area. The index considers market prices; however, it often underestimates them. For this reason, some Vietnamese students commented that there are cases where residents who are not satisfied with the price oppose evacuation in Vietnam.

In all countries except Myanmar, land and a building are considered different forms of immovable property. In those countries, the combined price of land and a house is compensation for the owner's loss. The value of a house is included in compensation for land in Myanmar.

(2) Compensation for a tenant

A tenant can directly receive compensation for relocation from a land expropriator in Cambodia, Thailand, and Japan. However, this does not mean that a tenant cannot claim the contractual liability from his owner. He can terminate a lease contract and claim compensation for damages caused by the termination of the contract.

The moderator commented that in this scheme, especially in Japan, a tenant sometimes receives a double payment, one from a land expropriator and one from an owner. It is a legal issue because a tenant then receives more than he loses from land appropriation.

A Vietnamese student was concerned that the owner has no contractual liability because a breach of contract cannot be attributed to him. The moderator asked the student about land expropriation which can potentially happen all the time, which is not the responsibility of the owner. Thus, there is a possible risk. What measures can the tenant take to ensure livelihood reconstruction?

A student from Hanoi explained that the government is responsible for paying the tenant compensation for lost livelihood according to a decree issued in 2017. A Cambodian student commented that a tenant's compensation may be limited to the fees related to a transfer. Thai students confirmed that currently, the government is responsible for compensating relocation, however, in her opinion, it should expand further.

(3) Compensation for possessors

Possessors, N1 to N10 live in a building on land without a land title. It has debated whether a developer can evict them without compensation. There were two questions: (1) whether a developer needed to compensate possessors; (2) if yes, whether the developer is responsible for paying the fees for relocation. The status of possessors may be different in each country. The moderator firstly confirmed the situation with participants.

A student from Ho Chi Minh City stated that the possessor issue is difficult and challenging to solve. Theoretically, the government does not need to compensate possessors without legal documents. However, in reality, they strongly oppose eviction. Therefore, the government pays little money to possessors after all.

A Thai student introduced the situation in her country. Previously, possessors needed to have written evidence to prove their right to possession, but the rule has changed. According to the new rule, relevant government agencies check whether people possess the land or not and try to prove their rights. It is because the previous law was complicated. The Thai system regards legal documents as important. People who have a document can go to a court to request a petition. Prescription can be an option for possessors, however, possession over 10 years is a requirement for prescription according to Thai civil and commercial law, but also certification is necessary.

A Cambodian student's comments focused more on the reality of possessors. She said N1 to N10 may start possession prior to a landowner appearing. However, land ownership is determined by a land title, not when the possession starts. Possessors do not have any means to challenge a landowner. She explained that this is considered a human rights problem in Cambodia.

The moderator confirmed that it is very difficult to determines who should be compensated for land acquisition. Compensation for land acquisition is compensation for the land. Thus, the landowner is the qualified person. However, it is also challenging to prove ownership of land. There is room for paying compensation to possessors to enhance social justice.

(4) Cultural rights of indigenous people

A discussion began about how each country treats ethnic groups and their interests. The moderator firstly introduced a recent Japanese case involving Ainu people, an ethnic group that lives in Hokkaido, the northern part of Japan, and is officially recognized as an "indigenous people" by 2019 legislation[13].

A Hanoi student introduced the decree which defines "minority people." and says that "minority" means "less than majority population." 80% of the Vietnamese population are Kinh ethnics. Thus, another ethnic group are protected as indigenous people. She also shared the ratification of international treaties in Vietnam. Vietnam is a member of the International Covenant on Civil and Political Rights, but it has not amended protocol number 1, yet.

A Thai student stated that in Thailand, the situation of ethnic minority groups is almost the same as in Vietnam. Another Thai student commented that there is a new trend in his country. He explained how the Supreme Court of Thai decided about community rights. Communities just have won two administrative cases, but he suggested that the State gradually pays attention to collective rights.

The class confirmed the United Nations Declaration on the Rights of Indigenous Peoples. However, it is not a convention and has no binding force, although it influences many countries' legislation, especially in terms of the informed consent of indigenous people. It seems that international rules create new domestic laws. The moderator commented that the recent Japanese Ainu law change is one of the cases illustrating how international trends change domestic situations. Japan has not paid attention to the rights of indigenous people for a long time,

---

[13] Act on Promotion of Policies to Realize the Society that Respect Dignity of Ainu (アイヌ の人々の誇りが尊重される社会を実現するための施策の推進に関する法律), passed and promogulated in April, 2019. Full text (Japanese) is available from the House of Councilor, https://www.sangiin.go.jp/japanese/johol/kousei/gian/198/pdf/s0801980241980.pdf (last accessed in January 10th, 2020).

Students Discussion

although it has established a new law.

Following the discussion of cultural rights, the moderator raised a summary question about how people's rights are protected concerning the rule of law. He commented that the word "law" appearing in the context of the rule of law means a "good" law, rather than simply passing through the Diet or Congress. However, what is a "good" law, and who decides "goodness"? Do rights create a law or a law create rights? These terms are not identical and may change in each country. He concluded that a consideration of the political, economic and social situation in each country is necessary to better understand the rule of law and how to improve the situation in each country.

3. Findings

It was the second multilateral and first law discussion that focused on the public law field. In terms of educational methodology, presentations and discussion styles made it easy to conduct comparative law study in a multilateral classroom. The program was delivered during an intensive law study program but could be used in a daily comparative law classroom and international classrooms.

In law study terms, students can easily notice and find the difference between legal systems by themselves after another country has made a presentation. This is because questions on the common topic include objects of comparative law. Students who notice the differences naturally ask other students why they adopt a different legal system. Students are then asked to explain the purpose or background of their country's legal system. Each student's awareness creates voluntary and lively communication, and enables a rich discussion of comparative law study.

Moreover, it enhances students' knowledge of another country's legal systems. This characteristic emerged during discussions about legal frameworks surrounding immovable properties. For example, the Japanese legal system treats land and a house as separate immovable properties. Japanese students learn that in some countries, such as France and Germany, a house is treated as a property attached to land in universities. However, this is little more than knowledge. By listening to presentations from Myanmar that introduced the same immovable property scheme as France and Germany, Japanese students recognized differences in legal practice as an actual feeling.

4. Conclusion

As confirmed in Part 3, the common topic is one of the useful methods for comparative law study and is especially effective in international classrooms. Although students' legal systems and backgrounds are different, they can still join in a discussion. However, some points remain in need of improvement.

The first point is that the development of comparative law discussion. Students could find and realize the difference of the legal system by themselves in the program. However, to develop a comparative legal debate, a recognition of reasons for differences of legal systems, alongside knowing differences between the systems is necessary. A fruitful group discussion can be a solution. A rich discussion may trigger student interest and may lead to students' continuous interest, and research in comparative law study. However, one issue raised was that the quality of discussion may change due to the skill of the moderator.

The second improvement would involve fostering a moderator who can facilitate students' discussion. The discussion of the common topic requires the ability to organize and understand various legal ideas from different countries. A moderator needs to understand student intentions and share their ideas with other participants. Highly skilled communication is required. University teachers regularly teach and research law but their daily activities are not enough to nurture the skills required for a common topic moderator. Moderating the common topic could develop the skills required to facilitate discussion.

With increased use, the content of common topic discussions and moderator skills will become more developed, and will become more useful as a general education method for comparative law study in the future.

INDEX

ABOUT KEIGLAD

KEIGLAD - Keio Institute for Global Law and Development

Keio Institute for Global Law and Development (KEIGLAD) was established for the purpose of assisting the promotion of international exchange and international cooperation among researchers, students, and staffs for legal study and legal education. KEIGLAD will promote the concerned projects as follow:

- Promotion of the Program for Asian Global Legal Professions (PAGLEP)
- Collection of information on the concerned comparative law
- Collection of information on the method of legal education
- Provision of materials for legal education
- Provision of information and support for foreign students who will study at Keio Law School and Keio Law School students who will study abroad
- Promotion of the concerned symposiums and research meetings
- Publication of working papers
- Other matters concerned with objectives of KEIGLAD

Through these activities, KEIGLAD aims to contribute to the promotion of "Law-Ubiquitous Society", in which Anyone can access to justice Anywhere and Anytime.

ABOUT THE AUTHORS

Isao Kitai
Professor, Dean, Keio University Law School, Japan

Tastuhiko Yamamoto
Professor, Keio University Law School, Japan

Phan Thi Lan Huong
Deputy Head, International Cooperation Department, Hanoi Law University, Vietnam; Head, Representative Office of Nagoya University in Vietnam

Luu Duc Quang
Lecturer of Law, Faculty of Law, University of Economics and Law, Vietnam National University in Ho Chi Minh city, Vietnam

Lien Dang Phuoc Hai
Lecturer of Law, Faculty of Law, University of Economics and Law, Vietnam National University in Ho Chi Minh city, Vietnam

Meas Bora
President, Cambodian University for Specialties, Cambodia

Noppadon Detsomboonrut
Assistant Professor, Faculty of Law, Thammasat University, Thailand

Myint Thu Myaing
Professor, Head, Department of Law, University of Yangon, Myanmar

Khin Phone Myint Kyu
Professor, Department of Law, University of Yangon, Myanmar

Hiroshi Matsuo
Professor, Keio University Law School; Director, Keio Institute for Glabal Law and Development (KEIGLAD), Japan

Hitomi Fukasawa
Researcher, KEIGLAD, Japan

MEXT/JSPS Re-Inventing Japan Project (Type B: ASEAN) FY 2016
文部科学省　平成 28 年度大学の世界展開力事業（ASEAN 地域における大学間交流の推進）
タイプ B 採択プログラム

How Public Law Is Taught in Asian Universities
Programs for Asian Global Legal Professions Series IV

2020 年 2 月 21 日　初版第 1 刷発行

編　者―――――KEIGLAD
発行者―――――KEIGLAD
　　　　　　　（慶應義塾大学大学院法務研究科グローバル法研究所）
　　　　　　　代表者　松尾　弘
　　　　　　　〒 108-8345　東京都港区三田 2-15-45
　　　　　　　TEL 03-5427-1574
発売所―――――慶應義塾大学出版会株式会社
　　　　　　　〒 108-8346　東京都港区三田 2-19-30
　　　　　　　TEL 03-3451-3584　FAX 03-3451-3122
装　丁―――――鈴木　衛
組　版―――――株式会社 STELLA
印刷・製本――中央精版印刷株式会社
カバー印刷――株式会社太平印刷社

©2020　KEIGLAD
Printed in Japan ISBN978-4-7664-2660-1
落丁・乱丁本はお取替致します。